Destiny Defined

We Did It R Way

Destiny Defined
We Did It My Way

Dr. Terri Drummond

Dr. Kathyleen Gamble-Wyatt

Dr. Nicoa Garrett

Dr. Phenessa A. Gray

Angela Malone, MA

Dr. J. Sabrina Simmons

Foreword by
Gwenevere Cisero Brinkley

Jacksonville, Florida, USA

For information about bulk purchases and/or to bring the authors to your live
event please contact us at (904)357-0057 or
contactus@wediditrway.com

Library of Congress Cataloging-in-Publication Data

ISBN 978-1-08-228402-1

PRINTED IN THE UNITED STATES OF AMERICA

Book design by Franklin Givens
Cover photography by James Schlefstein
Editor Rebecca Salome

This book is dedicated to all those who dare to discover what their 'R' is. We believe in you. We support you. We are cheering you on as you walk in your own *Destiny DeFined*...Do It Your Way!

Acknowledgments

Nova Southeastern University (NSU)–NSU's Jacksonville Campus has been instrumental in supporting *Destiny DeFined*. We are appreciative to the Campus Leadership and Staff for allowing us to meet and collaborate throughout this project. We are grateful for this opportunity to partner with you. Nova Southeastern University Staff: Brooke Goehring, Dr. Susan Forbes, Jacksonville, FL Site Leaders, EDD Peer Support Group & Education Club.

Rebecca Salome – A special thanks to Rebecca for coaching and consulting *Destiny DeFined* through this fantastic book journey. Your ability to review, synthesize, and streamline the writing process is priceless. We believe the introduction is an example of your labor of love and thorough understanding of your clients. We are tremendously grateful for your wisdom and up-close and personal touch with the team.

Marlanah Steven – It is better to give than to receive...Acts 20:35. Thank you, Marlanah for giving your precious time with the love in your heart for the written word. Your grace and guidance in finalizing this project were greatly appreciated.

Catherine O'Brien – A special thanks to Cathy for your fantastic support during our doctoral education journey. We appreciate you!

R Way

I had the pleasure of meeting the authors in 2013 as we began our doctoral journey. I'll never forget the day we received feedback from our professor on our first written assignment. My assignment was returned to me by the faculty member, indicating that not one thing in my paper was accurate–not one. He gave me an opportunity to resubmit a corrected paper. That evening, I called my doctoral sisters whom I just met four weeks earlier and I cried on the phone. I mean I shed big crocodile tears, snorting and all. I could not believe that my assignment was returned! For a minute, there was complete silence on the phone, but then one person spoke up and began to encourage me by letting me know that it would be okay. Then another chimed in that her assignment had also been returned. In fact, all of our assignments had been returned. I was in good company.

It was moments like what I just described that got me through the doctoral program. I am forever grateful for the love, support, and slaps upside the head the authors of this book gave me during the doctoral process. It is rare that you come across a group of women working toward the same goal who lift one another up and push them to the finish line. Our relationship has evolved from women who happened to be pursuing the same degree to family.

I consider each one of them my sisters, and I am so proud of the work they are doing to encourage other women on their journey by sharing their stories. I love you all. Y'all are some BBBs!

—Dr. April D. Murdaugh
Colleague

Contents

RISE

Gwenevere Cisero Brinkley, MA

Foreword

"Whoever renders service to many puts himself in line for greatness–great wealth, great return, great satisfaction, great reputation and great Joy."

—*Jim Rohn*

We are destined to be who we are from the very beginning of our existence; we just don't know who that is or how we'll get there. Life experiences and struggles help to form what that will look like; however, until we take our last breath, the journey is not over. The question is often asked of a child, "What do you want to be when you grow up?" Common responses are a medical doctor, lawyer, teacher, nurse, policeman, or fireman. However, as adults, we often ask the question automatically of every child we know and don't pay much attention to their answer—except to say: "Well, work hard, and you'll succeed." Very seldom do we discuss the actual road they will travel to get there. Most youngsters probably don't imagine in their wildest dreams they could actually have Ed.D. or Ph.D. after their name and be called "Doctor." Yet, that is the beauty of the words found in these pages. Even as I write this foreword, it is my destiny to do so. No, I haven't published a book, and I'm not famous, at least not yet, but I am honored to tell you about the authors of this book. It is their humility and their desire to elevate, inspire, and encourage others and each other that has resulted in *Destiny DeFined: We Did It R Way.*

So how did I come to this place? There I was—the home nest was empty, and my role in building a company from the ground up was over. What now? Trying to figure out what God has planned next for you can be a lonely, confusing time. Then (miraculously as usual), a voice said, "Gwen, we want you to be our project manager." These dynamic women extended their hands to bring me along on this part of the journey. No interview, no resume—just seeing "something" in me that was needed at exactly this time. I would later learn that the "something" was called "quiet power." God has a way, while you are waiting for your next assignment from Him, to give you just what you need to prepare for it.

Initially, I was approached by one of the authors about joining the journey of pursuing a doctoral degree. By then, I was engrossed in the start of the new nonprofit and did not have the bandwidth to add anything else to my plate.

However, I supported my friend's endeavor every step of the way. I remember being invited to a dinner to meet the other doctors. Some were already conferred, and others were working on their dissertations. As they introduced themselves, they explained individually what their respective dissertations entailed. They were all pursuing degrees in organizational leadership, tackling such issues as "Effects of Mentoring on Career Advancement for Women and People of Color" and "Front-End Analysis on the Perceived Correlation Between Organizational Leadership and Student Success." This inspired group, who decided to develop their own support system to help each other through the process of getting a doctorate, was a new concept for me and I was impressed.

Yet, still today, more than a half-century after the Civil Rights movement, strong, independent Black women must always be aware of the necessity to walk that delicate balance between needing support and the deeply imprinted fear of being vulnerable to judgment. As a privileged helper, honored to play a part in this book, I've learned, personally and through working with these educated and experienced leaders, that you will experience various emotions: elation, lack of confidence, sense of not being enough, and ultimately fear of failure. This is bound to be true when we undertake any endeavor where the work is hard, and the reward is worth it. Without a good support system at home, work, or school, it will be a fight for your sanity—possibly for your life!

This collection of important stories/essays is relatable and inspiring. Each is unique, and the author approaches her story in her own way. One account reads like a fireside chat and another reads like a drama.

I am in awe of Dr. Nicoa Garrett's traumatic experience, dealing with the impact of divorced parents at an early age. I admire the crucial mother role Dr. Terri Drummond had to take on—before she really had a clue about how the world-at-large worked. I'm inspired by both Dr. Kathyleen Gamble-Wyatt, who would learn so deeply the value of a good family support system, and future Dr. Angela Malone, who would forge her personal pain into her "Why Factor." Then, there's Dr. Phenessa A. Gray, who became her authentic self by overcoming learning disabilities and abuse. Finally, Dr. J. Sabrina Simmons, who had to press through the end of her program while dealing with what would turn out to be a natural and spiritual loss. They didn't allow their trials and tribulations to make them crawl up in a hole and die. They used their experiences as a catalyst to spark them into their destiny. These pages are filled with life lessons learned, wisdom and tools to encourage you to keep your eyes on the prize and never give up for you are not alone. As they *Rise* to the challenges set before them and put those challenges behind them, they each gained an inner strength that would put their "R" in *We Did It R Way*. What's your "R"?

It would be easy to view a group of Black females who have achieved this kind of success as snobbish and aloof. I have come to regard each one of them highly because they are direct but caring and professional but down to earth. Furthermore, they are so generous in their commitment to one another.

This book marks the women's goal to offer encouragement and support for anyone—no matter what field, career, aspiration, and no matter how high and big the dream—to reach for the stars.

It is not enough to say that I am honored to have been able to be the project manager for this powerful endeavor. I am so grateful that my "quiet PowHer" is the kind of spirit needed to foster a project of this nature. I have and treasure my deep desire to be a part of these women coming into their full potential. The mission now, and we do choose to accept it, is to reach as many women and men with the heartfelt and unique stories of this extraordinary circle of inspired women—the founders of *Destiny DeFined*. Just maybe one day, I will decide to tell more of my own story too!

Gwenevere Cisero Brinkley, Project Manager
(Affectionately referred to by the Ladies as "Dr. PM")

Introduction

Poised, determined, courageous, and phenomenal! Who would have ever thought that these six girls would be changing the environment of every room, arena, and territory entered by each of them with grace, grit, and an "I-can-do" attitude! It's funny how thoughts change over time about growing up from being a little girl and evolving into an extraordinary woman. For some, odds were stacked against them, and for others, bravery may have escaped them. However, there is one factor that is known with certainty: Each of their journeys definitely had twists and turns.

Just imagine, on any given elementary school yard there is happy chaos and noise—a playground ringing with the loud screams of kids playing familiar games like hopscotch, jump rope, or hide-and-seek. Perhaps, children are lining up to go down the slide or do hand-over-hand on the ladder bars. Oh, and let's not forget Miss Mary Mack and Rockin' Robin. And there's almost definitely a group of five or six girls banded together to chase the boys and prove they are as tough or tougher. Playground monitors and teachers stand around gazing with a watchful eye with hopes that everyone is playing fair and no one gets hurt. After all, these precious little people are under their care, and the adults are charged with helping to shape their future. Ironically, no one – not teachers, parents, grandparents, or pastors – really knows who or what these children will grow up to be. And, certainly neither do the children.

The above is a fictional scenario, but only because it doesn't refer to a specific child or group. Rather, it gives a general picture of young children on playgrounds all over this country. What you are about to read are the true stories of girls who didn't actually know one another in elementary school. Nearly three decades later, as young women, we came together in an intimate and powerful group to help each other succeed in accomplishing our dreams. We found that we shared dreams centered on continuing the education we had started as little girls. By now, we had all learned that, with the freedoms of adulthood also came the responsibility for carving our paths to the highest degree of formal education—a doctorate.

We believe that the personal insights we gained, and the candor with which we tell our stories of growing up, will resonate with many of you who have already envisioned and maybe even planned crystal-clear dreams about your future.

We support you and hope that our book will add even more power to your determination to succeed in whatever area or endeavor you choose. And we have come together in agreement to ask that God guide you on your path and give you the strength to overcome all obstacles and push through any barriers that may arise.

Particularly important to all of us is the commitment to those young women and men of Generations X and Z, as well as the Millennials (Gen Y), who might have experienced such difficult circumstances, rendering you unable to consider the possible goals and dreams you can achieve. You may not have thought yet about how you want your future to unfold or how far and high you can fly. Some of you may feel lost and even believe that adulthood is not something to look forward to. We hope our stories will show that "we've been there and done that," and we understand.

On the other hand, for so long, women have been pitted against each other—forced into fighting over the minimum opportunities and resources we felt we had a right to. No matter how things became this way, we know that seeking selfish gain without regard for others is not necessary. In fact, it actually keeps us from becoming a unified source of strength and wisdom that can change this divisive view and change the world as well.

All of the women in our stories are visionaries, and dreamers too, but we don't engage in wishful thinking; there's a huge difference between the two! We don't spend our time wondering about the "what ifs" when it comes to planning our futures. Instead we ask, "What will happen when...?"

- What will happen when we throw caution to the wind and start making our own rules in our own way?
- What will happen when we use the power within us to empower those around us?
- What will happen when we evoke our inner beauty, strength, and uniqueness to demolish the fairytale lives that a majority of us did not experience, and instead, create a world of unity and strength?

And, finally, perhaps the most important question of all:

- What will happen when all women and girls (no matter the age) grasp this vision and join together to make it happen?

We want you to know there's no limit if you truly want to become the best you can be. There are pathways that have already been traveled, tools that have been developed, and, most importantly, mentors who are waiting and eager to help you. We can assure you that the power of building relationships and a sustaining network to support each of us and you too are essential. And also very doable– as we found out!

That's how we evolved into a circle of committed women who set out on our paths equipped with self-determination and spirit to effect change not only in our academic community, but also in the wider world. During this journey we "doctoral sisters" used a push/pull strategy to ensure that each of our educational goals was accomplished. As one of us was pushed to get to her goal, she reached back to pull another sister forward.

Our founding members include educators, counselors, consultants, entrepreneurs, a realtor, ministers, and authors. And happily, we are all Women of God. We see ourselves as a small but powerful unit willing to "go out there" and explore new territory in order to open pathways for other younger women to come into their own power. Our support circle became a symbol for other women to band together to build a similar sisterhood connection.

Our voyage, as revealed in our book, is about unapologetically beautiful Black ladies who created more than an education club; it's about the great, transcending relationships we continue to have today. Our stories tell how each of us overcame life's obstacles throughout our mission to achieve a doctoral degree. We hope you will relate to and feel the joyful (and sometimes heartbreakingly painful) experiences that are intertwined with priceless and exhilarating moments. There is no doubt that we each saw and experienced true miracles along the way!

As women of color, we have made a conscious decision to embrace, support, encourage, and love one another. This is not an exclusionary decision, but rather one that is aimed toward building the foundation that we feel will put us on a par with anyone (woman or man) of any ethnic and cultural background to advance our opportunities and goals. Throughout this endeavor, we have formed a truly vital and unbreakable bond. This tightly woven net of strength has held us as we survived hardships—internal turmoil, times of high stress, bumps on the academic trail, loss of a failed relationships, family changes and misfortunes, and even the deaths of loved ones.

We, the sisters of *Destiny DeFined*, have more than "been there" for each other; we have served as mentors, seamlessly switching back and forth in this necessary and sometimes life-saving role. There have been so many blessings on this journey, we've lost count. But every day, we remember to honor ourselves and each other, and to thank God that He brought us together to make a contribution. We hope that our stories inspire thousands of our sisters and brothers who are willing to strive for their dreams and turn them into a joyful reality.

R E A L
Dr. Terri Drummond

Chapter 1

Double ALL THE WAY Down

"When the odds are against you JUMP and double ALL THE WAY down."

— *Dr. Terri Drummond*

As a child, I was inquisitive, resourceful, responsible, and reliable—the "acting" head of the household. My mother worked more than one job in an effort to keep food on the table. Like many other children in my neighborhood, I grew up in a single-parent household. I was a latchkey kid who tried to understand big-world issues from the frame of reference of someone who had not seen beyond her own community. In elementary school, I was often reminded during black history month of Martin Luther King Jr., and his dream. I too had dreams. My dreams were BIG, but my desire to help my family and my community were so much bigger. I sensed that my life had a purpose, but I never actually saw what success or fulfillment looked like. In my mind, I knew it didn't look like me. I didn't learn until much later in life that somehow the teachings during black history month silenced the "Dr." in front of Martin Luther King Jr.

When I was sixteen, I joined the stereotyped group of "black high-school dropouts," but not for the reasons most people would have thought. I was afforded an opportunity to enter the workforce early, and I jumped at it. Even though it was a low-paying job in a call center, I was making more money than many of the adults in my community, and I was making it honestly. I worked for years in that position and transferred with the same organization to another call center.

Fast forward to age 22, an event occurred that proved to be pivotal in my story. Now, I was a single mother with a newborn, and still a high school dropout. One day, I took my son in for a checkup. It seemed like the nurse, although I could see that she was being thorough, was taking too long. I became impatient. She was young, black, and getting on my nerves. I asked her if she could please go and get the doctor. She looked up at me and giggled. "I am the doctor," she said with a cheerful smile. I'm pretty sure my mouth dropped open; I was speechless. I stood there frozen, but, for some reason, I distinctly remember wanting to touch her face. For the first time in my life, I saw a black doctor. Up to this point, I had no idea they existed; it had never occurred to me that a doctor could be black. That was the turning point for my life. At that moment, I realized the narrative regarding the intellectual capacity and learning abilities of people who looked like me was false.

The images that had been shown to me in public school were of slavery and Martin Luther King Jr. I didn't know anything about my ancestors. For that matter, I knew very little about my dad. As I began to search out people who were hiding in plain sight—the upper echelon of the black community—I realized they didn't live in my community, but they were there. Somewhere.

As a few years passed, I continued to work hard, and it began to pay off. I changed employers and was eventually promoted into management. Equipped with only a GED, a desire to win, and the ability to influence people, I made the company millions. I bled for the company. I often worked from open to close. During that time, my relationship with my child suffered. What should have been "mommy time" was spent in the office working long and hard because of my fear of food insecurity. My focus was on fulfilling physiological needs while abandoning love and belonging. My focus was my grind.

While I worked, my mother became the caregiver to my child in the same way that I had been the caregiver to her children. Our roles had reversed. After years at the company, I was asked to interview—as the only internal candidate—for a regional management position. I wasn't exactly sure what that really meant or what it would entail, but I agreed to interview. Afterward, I was told I was a proven candidate and there was no question about my skillset or ability to perform in the role. The problem, though, was that I had no formal education. They explained that the candidate they selected came from a regional management position like mine, but also had a college degree. I was still excited about having been the only internal candidate asked to interview, but now I began to think, and think, and think some more. In the middle of the night I paced the floor thinking. The next day, on my break, I walked the parking lot—thinking. On the drive home, thinking consumed the time I would normally spend singing at the top of my lungs. I thought about my life in its entirety. I had given everything to the organization, leaving nothing for myself. I had even abandoned the relationship with my son to ensure the organization could see my worth. I had equated working hard with success. In my mind, success meant that, eventually, I would be able to change the course of life for myself and my child.

After lots of tears, deep consideration, and hearing the voice that echoed over and over again, "You have no formal education," I decided to JUMP. I understood that, if I continued to work in a role that often required 12-hour days, I would never have the opportunity to get a higher education. I was at another critical decision point. The idea of quitting was reminiscent of my high school experience, and it scared me to death. After days of internal dialogue, I had reached a point of mental exhaustion. For the first time in my life, I had to confront my fears of financial insecurity and even homelessness. Literally shaking, I turned in my resignation. Suddenly, to my surprise, I felt free. I realized I was broken and broke, but I was free. The fears that had kept me working so hard were still present, but I also knew the skillset I had acquired over the years would serve to propel me into the next chapter in my life.

Soon after announcing my planned departure from the company, I was contacted by a headhunter, who had been provided my information. I interviewed and accepted the position, but this time, even though I was scared as hell to try and negotiate, I set boundaries. I said I would accept the offer if I was allowed to go to school (truth be told I would have accepted even if they had said no). I explained that I was on a mission toward higher education. My new employer agreed, and so the story begins...I earned my Bachelor's degree in Workforce Education and Management, a dual Master's degree in Human Resources Management and Development, and set out on the path to a Doctorate in Organizational Leadership. While I have many other designations, certificates, and credentials to my credit this is how my journey begins...

During the journey, I didn't fear failure. I had already been written off early on as a failure. The fact is I had nothing to lose. Failing didn't hurt. I found it interesting to fail. It allowed me to explore areas of weakness and perfect them. I distinctly remember being hired by a temporary agency on a short-term assignment as a switchboard operator at the age of 23. They felt like it was a great fit because of my work in telecommunications. By lunchtime, the agency terminated my employment. To be fair, they should have; the entire switchboard lit up at once and I felt like I was being pranked. I leaned over to the big office next to me and asked while hysterically laughing if I was being pranked—the termination call followed quickly thereafter.

I realized that sometimes people want you to fail—it's a part of your journey and theirs. In fact, my failures often allowed others an opportunity. I also realized, sometimes it's necessary to laugh out loud at yourself. It's necessary to take a deep-down belly laugh—a fall on the floor with tears in your eyes type of laugh—a hysterical, I can't stop laughing type of laugh. At some point, I adopted an attitude of positivity and subscribed to the idea that fear and faith cannot exist in the same space. I started pushing myself to the edge of my known capabilities and leaning way over the edge reaching, often blindly, for the teacher to appear. This method has not failed me; the teacher has always shown up.

I realized along the way that it is necessary to research and understand the real stories of our forefathers and mothers. I am still working on understanding this truth. Although I now have an expanded understanding beyond slavery and Dr. Martin Luther King Jr., I have very limited knowledge of where I came from and the queens and kings that are likely a part of my lineage. When I hear stories or read in books altered facts of history, I am reminded, "One must study to show thyself approved." When I realized that people who look like me are inventors, investors, doctors, lawyers, change makers, philanthropist and the like and have always been, it sparked an awakening. This understanding ignited passion.

I am passionate about people. All people. I have a special place in my heart for disadvantaged/vulnerable populations. I currently serve on the board for a mental health organization and volunteer advocating for abused and neglected children. I focus on programs for children who suffer from mental illness. My past volunteer work included advocating for persons with disabilities and domestic violence victims. Although I served in this role as a volunteer, advocating for those who often find difficulty in advocating for themselves due to capacity or other reasons, it was one of the most important aspects of my life.

My journey has been one of challenges and significant triumphs. I've learned that people will let you down and they will absolutely fail you. I have also learned there are people who will build you up. It is necessary to recognize early who those people are. Once you identify which tribe they are in, govern yourself accordingly. Let your haters become your motivators. Shine on. Although I have addressed this in a very simplistic way, as women in business, especially when you are a six-figure earner, you must understand haters will hate. When they do, don't worry—go high! There is no doubt in my mind that there is an opportunity divide for women and minorities. I can speak as an expert for both of these populations. The opportunity divide exists in my opinion because of the lack of knowing that the opportunity exists and the conditioning many of us have been exposed to.

I remember working for a global bank in a non-managerial role. I saw a job posting for an executive-level job. It was several positions above that of my manager and director. Just for kicks, I applied and shared that I had done so with my co-workers. We laughed incessantly, and I remember saying, "They might not give me the job, but they'll say my makeup looks good."

A week or so passed when I received a call to interview from a Senior Vice President (SVP). I was stoked! What had started off as a joke would serve once again to change the course of my life. The interview went very well. I wasn't nervous at all. I had nothing to lose because I already had a job. When the SVP called, he told me that he was new to his role within the department and needed training on internal systems. Because I worked for a different business unit, I didn't use the system he needed to learn. He said if I had knowledge of the system, the decision would have been very different. So, I didn't get the job but the whole experience gave me a shot of confidence in my worth. I WAS HYPED!

As fate would have it, I decided to JUMP again and, this time, it was into a Vice President (VP) position with a different organization. Retrospectively, it occurred to me that, in my younger years, I would often go for low-hanging fruit. Experience has taught me to take the low-hanging fruit and use it to aim for the top of the tree. Gain the skills, but do not believe the limits others set for me. I asked myself this guiding question; "Who was I, before I was cognizant of what the world told me I should be?"

I've found my professional niche is that of a leader. But it has become equally important to spend time—to catch up on years missed—with my son and the rest of my family. My career has come full circle. Those early years working in call centers set the foundation for me to truly know the field and to work with diverse people of varying socio-economic backgrounds. I was fascinated with how call centers operated—especially the people who work in the cubicles: their stories, their emotions, their plight. My doctoral dissertation is on "The Relationship Between Emotional Labor and Job Satisfaction and Its Effect on Intention to Quit and Quitting Within Call-Center Environments." I have sown many seasons in this industry and want to leave a stamp on it, because it was one of the first opportunities given to me. We have a lot of work to do in that industry to expand our knowledge and fill gaps in the literature.

I hope that something in my experiences will resonate with you. It is never too late to walk in your destiny, and always keep it *Real*.

A few special tips to my younger readers:

- Take the limits off. As Rory Vaden, bestselling author of *Take the Stairs* said, "Do it scared."

- Don't worry about what others say. The limitations are for them— not you.

- Remember your past and use it to create your future. Our circumstances and environment help to shape how we see the world and the people and things in it. So, step out of your comfort zone.

- Explore. If you can jump on a plane, do it. If you can't, go drive around in a different neighborhood—the landscape just might be different. It's important to see something other than what you know or have been told.

- Set excellence as your goal. You don't need permission to be great. Don't procrastinate, and don't get caught up doing busy work. Focus on what matters.

- Set boundaries. Identify your core values and stick to them.

The Journey to My Doctorate:
A Written Documentary

"Leadership is like a panicle of rice because at the height of the season, at the height of its power, it is beautiful, it is green, it nourishes the world, it reaches for the heavens; but right before the harvest it bends over with great gratitude and humility to touch the earth from where it came."

— *Joseph Byaruhanga*

The Beginning of the Doctoral Journey!!!

A quick disclaimer: I am not a formal teacher; nevertheless, I am an educator. So, I ask you to please bear with me as I try very hard to take off my educator's hat and put on my favorite PJ's, sip my favorite tea, English Breakfast to be exact, and share my story...

Atlanta, Georgia, is where it all began. Yes, I am a "Grady Baby!" Those familiar with the area will understand my humble beginnings. I was fortunate to have two loving parents, two big brothers (Langston and Carl), and a neighborhood of people who spent their day catering to the only little girl on the block. When I was about five, our family moved to southeast Georgia to care for my aging grandfather, who only lived a year after we arrived. On a positive note, I was able to attend the first public kindergarten in the beautiful, historical city of Brunswick, Georgia. Going through the public school system, in the early 1970s, I experienced a lot of rezoning. As a result, I attended three different elementary schools in five years. Despite the continuum of rezoning, I managed to maintain exceptional academic attainments and became one of the principal's favorite students. I'm not sure why. Okay, maybe that's not totally true. I spent an excessive amount of time in the principal's office, due to my gift of constant communication and not enough instructional material to keep me busy all day. That is my side of the story and I am sticking to it until "death do us part." In junior high school, I completed the awkward transition from "cute little dark chocolate girl with Indian-type hair" to a pimply-faced skinny body pre-teen, who still managed to be popular among her peers. I found my "verb" several times over: cheerleading, chorus, violin (not my best musical undertaking per my mother), clarinet, and finally basketball.

In the summer of 1980, I changed again, but this time, it wasn't quite so successful. I grew into a young lady physically, but mentally I was still a young girl, who thought boys were disgusting (including my brothers at times). My peers had already started dating and were sexually active, so their mothers took them to the public health department to receive birth control pills. I was emotionally lost, feeling weird, because I did not fit in with that part of their lives, but still really enjoyed our co-ed sandlot football and kickball games. Eventually, peer pressure won me over and I hooked up with an older boyfriend. Six months later, I was pregnant with a baby boy at the ripe ole' age of 14. We cried; yes, my mother and I cried together, until the tears dried up and we could muster enough strength to tell my father. My wonderful, committed parents offered to adopt the bundle of joy, so I could live a normal teenage life and attend Boston University, near my favorite aunt and uncle; I graciously declined. It was the best thing that could have happened to me at the least opportune time. I raised my son, Bruce, while my parents finished raising me.

The highlight of my senior year of high school was making the cheerleading team and being nominated by my high school peers as a homecoming queen contestant. I went on to graduate from high school with the class of 1984.

My doctoral aspirations began around this time, inspired by a 1980s popular sitcom featuring a positive African-American family in which the parents had achieved the academic title of "Doctor." I aspired to become Dr. Kathyleen Gamble one day, but only after my son and future children were grown.

I also wanted to be married like my parents, who started dating in junior high school and are still married after 58 years. I believed strongly in two-parent families, so I married Bruce's father at 17, only to be divorced at 20. I tried marriage again at 23; we brought two beautiful children, Brandon and Kathy, into the world. This phase of my life also ended in divorce, after 13 years of verbal and emotional abuse.

But, I never lost sight of my dream, and on August 31, 2016, I married the current love of my life and my new best friend, Steven B. Wyatt. On December 31, the same year, I was conferred as Doctor Kathyleen Gamble-Wyatt, with a degree in Education from Nova Southeastern University.

Modeling, Engaging, Noble, Tenacious, Omnipresent, *Relentless...* MENTOR!! WHEW, I get excited about it and I hope you will as well! Helping others achieve their dream through MENTORing. That acronym was not a prolific epiphany– it was just my way of explaining what I do every day as a MENTOR. My Christian belief and practice are grounded in "it is always better to give than to receive." It is the source of my passion and drive. Giving can take many forms in life, and I have chosen to give of my time, wisdom, and love to others as reverence to God—as my appreciation for what He has done for me, despite my imperfections and falling short of His glory on several occasions. Through it all, God continues to bless me, lead me, and guide me as I do the same for others.

I learned the spirit of giving and caring from my mother and mentoring others from my father. My father helped us by teaching us to help ourselves. Mentoring and helping others with life skills can have its challenges and, at times, may not seem rewarding or appreciated; however, as I continue in my practice, I find so much joy in giving unconditional love and support to others, without receiving a tangible token of appreciation. Instead, I get spiritual satisfaction from heeding the Word of God.

It gives me overwhelming tears (of joy) to have someone say that I was able to assist them in attaining their dreams, goals, or at a minimum, offer a word of encouragement. I myself have several purposeful mentors, all of them my seniors in age, who have a wealth of relevant wisdom that is key to my continued and unlimited future endeavors.

Knowledge is power. Ergo, I combine book knowledge, life lessons, and common sense to fuel my passion for internal peace, as well as foster love and peace in others.

Let's snuggle a little closer and talk about one of my plethora of imperfections—fear. What is life without some form of fear? Everything has its place and purpose. Even though I spend so much of my time helping others to overcome fear, I am afraid of competing. I get internal anxiety when completing a task that is competitive in nature, as I am passionate about everything I do. In school, I participated in sports, band, the performing arts, and fashion modeling. I never excelled at any of these activities. As I reminisce, I realize it's because I do not have a competitive nature. I enjoy whatever I am doing, but the minute it becomes seriously competitive, I lose interest and my skill level declines. Life has so many simple pleasures that fill my heart with joy that I choose to embrace more often than not, and if I receive a reward or recognition along the way, it's a bonus and not my purpose.

Disclaimer...this next section is the opinion of the author...the one and only Dr. Kathyleen Gamble-Wyatt; it is strictly my opinion, and I pray that you accept it in the spirit it is intended...

Racism, discrimination, and injustice have been a part of the human existence since biblical times. We are all descendants of the thoughts and ways of our forefathers and mothers; it will take many more generations of an anti-racist mindset to foster and live in true equality. I feel that millennials have made the most progress in bringing the concept of an equal societal coexistence to fruition. They have broadened communication among nationalities with the use of technology, especially social media. In doing so, they have formed their own understanding and expectations of their peers, which has catapulted the lessening of racism, discrimination, and injustice for their generation. They are no longer dependent on their grandparents' and parents' account of the past or view of the future.

Of course, we cannot ignore the past, because it is significant and relevant to the way we view, address, and ultimately eradicate discrimination, racial profiling, and injustice. These issues exist even at my level of education, but I find that it happens most often out of pure ignorance, jealousy, or retaliation for something in the past. How do I respond? I reveal, acknowledge, address, and educate!

Now we're getting more serious; I think I need a fresh cup of tea...

Change is inevitable: How do we adapt? What's Next? Yes, there are fewer opportunities for women and minorities in general to launch meaningful careers. First, let's examine why. A study of Women's history shows that we did not always work outside of the home, and if so, it was usually in someone else's home in a domestic role: cooking, cleaning, sewing, childcare, etc. As time went on, women slowly infiltrated the mainstream of employment, and due to a higher divorce rate, became the sole provider for their household. These circumstances launched the need for women to increase their net worth as a valuable part of the working-class economy.

African-American and Hispanics have both had the displeasure of being deemed able to be proficient only in jobs less desirable to Caucasians. The opportunity divide started many years ago when African-Americans in our country were slave labor. It continues with the "importation" (and deportation) of Mexicans into the United States.

What is the long-term solution to the problem of uneven opportunity in our society? First, be a part of the change you would like to see in others. Next, increase educational opportunities and training initiatives for women and minorities in the workforce. At present, both groups must over-qualify to compete in the job market, but I am optimistic this will continuously improve and create true equal employment opportunity in the United States. The final word is for my Christian readers: *Matthew 19:30* states, "The first will be last and the last will be first."

Teachable Moments

Chinese Proverb: "Give a man a fish and you feed him for a day: teach a man how to fish and you feed him for a lifetime"

-Maimonides

My daddy was a certified electrician by trade, and I believe he is the best father anybody could have. No, he is not perfect, but he's as close to it as possible by being a good husband and father to our family. He taught me to be calm and to be slow to speak, because people will be more attentive to what you are saying. He never raised his voice to us, but when he spoke, the world stood still and we listened. Yes, my brothers received occasional spankings, but this was on rare occasions. My father is one of Jehovah's Witnesses; in lieu of spanking us, the punishment was reading an encouraging Bible passage that would help us make better decisions in the future. In my case, I preferred a spanking—mostly (and kindly) given out by my mother when I was the guilty one. Treat and release, but no long-term effects!

My father taught me to be independent; anything I needed help with, he showed me how to do myself. When I asked a question, he told me to research the answer in the encyclopedia.

My loving, caring mother always put others before herself. She made very few friends outside of her siblings, and not until my siblings and I were in public school did she work outside the home. She was a Certified Nursing Assistant until retirement—still caring for others—but her focus has never stopped being the best wife and mother she could be. I awake daily inspired to walk in her footsteps.

The mirror: Self-reflection, as I continuously look back while persistently transitioning and moving forward in life's journey.

I think the words persistence and relentlessness are nearly the same or at least interwoven enough to be almost synonymous, as we navigate through life. And I would love to say that they became the building blocks of my own life through a miraculous epiphany, but they did not. I needed my parents to set a foundation of persistence. Then, my community "village" reinforced it by showing me that if I hit a road-block, I must find another path to travel.

I was never given limits on choosing what I wanted to accomplish; if I did not succeed in a particular extracurricular activity, my mother told me it was okay and asked, "What's next?" This great parenting and community support are responsible for any relentlessness I now have in overcoming obstacles.

A Note to Myself: Past, Present and Future

If God granted me a redo of my life, I would have tried to make a more informed choice of a soul mate. I was married twice by the age of 25, both times for the wrong reasons. As I hastened to have the relationship that my parents have, I didn't understand the dynamics of marriage—what characteristics I should look for in selecting a "Lifetime Partner" versus an "At This Time Partner." As a Christian, I have not and do not dwell over my past. I acknowledge that my path in life is predetermined, and I'm only able to create detours along the way. God's plan for my life will come to fruition in His time, and it will be done according to His will.

Another note I'd make would be about listening to the advice of those who have gone before you (e.g., talk to several married couples in depth). Listen and understand their stories before making a commitment. And, I'd add, "You don't have to hit a brick wall, if you pay attention!" In other words, listening to others did not keep me from experiencing challenges and making new mistakes. But, it helped me not repeat theirs and waste the invaluable gift of time. Time can be either well-spent or poorly spent on making unproductive decisions. I did a lot of the latter despite the wise words of my elders.

Potential Realized: As the only girl and the youngest child, I did not have to spend a lot of time doing for others. I was free to focus on becoming the best person I could be and working hard to achieve my personal goals; I was fortunate. Both of my parents attended college and learned a technical skill, which was a privilege in the 1940's and 1950's. I knew—that is, assumed—I would graduate from college, just like my parents, in order to position myself for a white-collar job and assist in providing a comfortable lifestyle for my future family. God has blessed me to achieve my goals through it all, and now I am driven to mentor and inspire others to meet their life long goals especially through furthering their education after high school.

Do Not Sleep on Your Dreams What advice do I want to leave to whomever I am blessed to MENTOR? Remain relentless, resilient, and engaged. Obtain and live "your" dream. I think of the words written by the late, great poet, Langston Hughes. Words that are relevant to all of us:

Harlem

What Happens to a Dream deferred?

Does it dry up

like a raisin in the sun?

Or fester like a sore—

and then run?

Does it stink like rotten meat?

Or crust and sugar over—

like a syrupy sweet?

Maybe it just sags

like a heavy load.

Or does it explode?

I hope that what I have written will inspire others, as I continue to be omnipresent in mentoring, writing, and speaking of my PowHerfullness—mine and other women as well.

(Yawn) Goodness! Writing in my PJ's makes me feel sleepy—but that's not the same as sleeping on your dreams! Thank you for staying with me, people, and reading my story. I'll end with praying that God will allow my life and legacy to continue for a while longer...

Acknowledgments

Thank you to my village of family, friends, neighbors, and very meaningful strangers for your continued outpouring of love and support.

A personal and continuous thank you to my dear parents, Carl and Rose Gamble, for being the example of true love, dedication and commitment. Thank you for your firm and patient guidance throughout the years. The both of you are the epitome of parenting under all circumstances.

To my loving husband, Steven, though we are still considered newlyweds, our mental history extends many years before we physically joined hands in holy matrimony. Thank you for your insight and editing of all my writing endeavors. May God continue to bless and guide us for eternity...Honey Bear and Doll Baby.

Big brother, Langston, many thanks for your strong but silent love and guidance, and most of all for the sacrifice of your time and finances in support of your sister.

To my younger brother, Carl II, you were the best brother babysitter ever with or without a choice. Thank you for giving me an appreciation for old black & white western movies. Thank you for bringing my awareness to recognizing and accepting the consequences and repercussions, both amiable and questionable, of my plethora of life choices, as I developed into Dr. Kathyleen Gamble-Wyatt.

My half-sister, Cheryl, we met later in life as adult women, but the joy of knowing that the sister I always longed for as a little girl did exist and we share very similar backstories; it's amazing.

My life, my loves, my heartbeats: To my children and grandchildren, I have set the bar and left a legacy. Please take the baton and run with it in the direction of your individual dreams, your faith, and your heart's desire with all my love, your mama a.k.a. mema.

R E S T

Dr. Nicoa Garrett

Chapter 3

Unstoppable

"We delight in the beauty of the butterfly, but rarely admit the changes it has gone through to achieve that beauty."

— *Maya Angelou*

I was eight and mad as hell!! My world had been turned upside down; my parents divorced, and the family was torn apart. I started shutting down the happy side of myself and letting anger determine my behavior. I figured, since no one else cared about how I was feeling, why should I let them know how hurt I was. My thought was, "If they don't care, I don't either." I was all alone in my own world, but I was not going to be quiet. I would fight and get the attention I wanted—good or bad, it didn't really matter.

My negative attitude got me kicked out of school more than ten times for fightin', cussin', and other unacceptable behavior. Eventually, my parents were told that if I got kicked out of school again, I would be barred from any school in the county. But I still didn't care; so much rage was built up inside me that consequences neither scared nor bothered me. It did cross my mind that if I went to a school for delinquents, those kids would probably beat my tail for breakfast, lunch, and a snack, but it still was not enough to make me change my ways.

I was not really hard-core or a thug, I was just hurting, and no one could see it. Most of my friends' parents did not want their daughters to hang around me because they thought I was sassy and a bad influence. I would hear people say things like, "She's too loud," or "She's a troublemaker," or "She'll be the first to get pregnant." As I am writing, I can still see some of the looks of disgust toward me from certain individuals. Not many people thought I would amount to anything. It didn't seem likely that things could change or get better, but, somehow, over time, I began to get my life together.

At the age of 13, I started making some major changes that included giving my life to God. I began attending a church that talked about faith and Jesus in ways I had never heard, such as "God promises to provide and take away hurt" and "You can do all things through Christ Jesus." I did not fully understand everything, but I knew I wanted whatever the pastor was talking about. I was overcome with curiosity and decided to try this Jesus thing for myself. When I did, I noticed an immediate change in the way I felt inside on a daily basis.

Over time, I found I was no longer angry. I started wanting to forgive, and my heart was beginning to soften toward others. It was in this process that I decided I needed and wanted something better for my life. So, I looked for and found positive activity outlets, people and places from which to receive help, encouragement, and something to lift my spirit. I joined my church youth choir and started reading the Bible and some self-help books for teens. During this process, I discovered my love for writing. I learned that journaling helped me to sort through areas of hurt and pain. Reading and writing about my personal feelings strengthened me to face my pain and anger, as well as to overcome it.

I finished high school and went off to college in another city. Just two weeks into the semester, I hit a potential roadblock. A professor told me I was not "college material," because I did not have the books for the class.

The actual issue was not my level of intelligence, but the fact that I had to wait for my financial aid request to clear. That eye-opening experience was the beginning of not only deciding either to shut negative people out of my life and avoid any negative situations, but better yet, to also transform the interactions and encounters into fuel for an already-burning fire of passion. The little girl, who had for so long been raging inside, was waiting, without even knowing it, for the right time and opportunity to begin evolving into the person God had already ordained her to be. It took a long time to go through the fire of pain to reach the fire of a vision filled with peace and happiness, but the wait was well worth it!

While in college full-time, I worked three part-time jobs. Each semester, I carried between 12 and 18 credit hours and each of the hours required more hours of homework. It was a true miracle that I found enough hours in the day to do what had to be done. I barely had enough money to afford rent, food, or buy new clothes. Any other personal or fun items were totally out of the equation. I was almost evicted from my apartment twice due to late payments. I had to appear in court due to a judgment entered against me for late rent payments. When it was my turn to stand before the judge, he asked, "Why aren't you paying your rent on time?" I responded, "I am a full-time student and I have three part-time jobs, but it's still not enough to cover everything." He asked if I could provide a list of my monthly expenses; I was able to document every single penny of expenses, including the tithes I paid from whatever money I made. "You pay tithes?" the judge asked. I answered, "Yes." He raised his head and his voice to the courtroom. "Throw this case out and remove it from the record. Young lady, I believe you're doing the best you can. Keep up the good work. I don't want to see you in here again." This was the beginning of me learning the priceless importance of God's grace and favor on my life. However, I still spent many days and nights wondering how I would make "ends meet" to pay bills or finish school with such limited funds. There were days I did not have even enough money or tokens for the bus, subway, or train to get to school.

One morning, as usual, I needed to be at school, but I did not have any money to get there. It was during mid-terms, and I could not afford to miss classes. What happened next, some may find hard to believe. I asked God to provide a way for me to get to school. The Holy Spirit spoke to me and said, "Walk to the bus stop and just wait." I protested, "I don't have any money or tokens." Nevertheless, I had learned enough about such things to not dare ignore what I had heard. So, I walked to the bus stop in the cold, snowy storm and waited with about five to six other people for the bus to arrive. The bus came, and the doors opened. I stood there wondering how to maneuver through the situation. I moved up the steps, pretending to reach inside my purse and search for money (that I knew I did not have). Before I could get very far into digging inside my purse, the driver said, "Just go" and put his hand over the top of the money dispenser. I told him I needed to pay for a transfer, and he said, "Okay," tore off a transfer, and just gave it to me. I went and sat down in my seat and cried like a baby while thanking God for at least ten minutes. This was another pivotal point in my faith walk with God. I was beginning to learn that, no matter how big or small my needs were, my God was continuously developing and creating a track record with me—letting me know that I will never have to worry about Him not coming to my rescue.

My college journey was beginning to open a whole new world of opportunities and possibilities that made me believe more and more in myself. It never dawned on me until just before graduation that I would be the first in my entire family to graduate from a four-year university or college. I was so proud of my accomplishment. After college, I obtained a good job in the financial industry. No one could have ever made me believe that I would work at any job dealing with numbers. I HATED MATH!!! But

I studied, prepared, and passed the test to receive my Series 6 and 63 mutual funds investment licenses. I started working in the financial industry and enjoyed it for almost 20 years. During this time, I worked for three well-known financial companies, and one of them paid for my Master's degree in Information Management & Technology. And, again, here comes God, showing up and demonstrating His love for me.

In 2009, I received a great severance package from a company that had been very good to my family and me for many years. The severance was so generous I did not have to work for quite some time. Corporate America had treated me well, but I decided I did not want to go back. I needed to follow my heart, which was being called to change disconnected systems in society that place underserved populations, such as women, children, and minorities, at a disadvantage. This was when I decided to pursue a doctoral degree in Organizational Leadership and Conflict Resolution. I wanted to be someone who was changing mindsets and rewriting narratives on policy and procedure. I have learned that change must begin with me first, and others will soon follow. The beauty in all of this is that barriers and walls were torn down demonstrating to others that they can accomplish their highest goals in life.

Looking back over the years, and the stages I went through, discovering more and more about who I truly am, I can see that my outlook on life had become altogether different than before. I no longer saw myself as a victim of shame, pain, and hurt. I started believing that I could accomplish anything and could have whatever I wanted. I noticed that I was still a fighter, but a different kind of fighter with a different purpose. Now, I saw myself as one who would never give up or quit. I realized I had the option to live and advance in life by seeing and thinking about myself through the eyes of God, which meant I was created to have dominion. This new perspective changed the course of my life forever.

For the first time, my true passion was exposed and clarified. This passion, which from then on would shape my ideas and actions, was to inspire greatness in others and impact families and communities. Doing so sparked a relentless determination in me to walk in the business of changing lives daily. I came to understand that I was created to intentionally cause others to have hope, to believe in and have faith in God and to use their God-given talents to win in life with confidence.

Once my passion was revealed to me, I had to learn to chase it, to keep various pathways open and accessible. My determination to overcome all obstacles, combined with the drive to achieve my goals, kept me grounded and focused in that process. My foundation to success lay in my tenacity to be gritty: to have the grit to grind, endure, and even to purposefully excel, regardless of whatever hand had been dealt to me. Finally, having a firmness of mind to remain focused on my natural, God-given talent was where I found the gold. The key to discovering my passion, then, was accepting my natural giftings: determination, drive, tenacity, focus, persistence, and most importantly, faith.

Passion, which had now become the centerfold of my new God-led life, inspired and motivated me to take a step back and figure out the answers to four questions:

1. What was I good at doing (strengths)?
2. What was I not good at doing (weaknesses)?
3. What drove me or made me happy (opportunities)?
4. What was I continuously doing that was NOT working (threats)?

As I mentioned before and cannot overemphasize, learning and understanding my natural gifting were paramount. Once I understood it, what was once a struggle became almost effortless because the work was naturally accomplished with ease and enlightenment. When I finally realized that what was naturally easy to me was my gift of excelling at life, I began to see increases in my accomplishments and successes directly tied to my giftings. Sadly, many people spend too much time in areas of non-talent or outside of their natural gifts. The good news is that there is always time and room for change. I can speak from the heart of personal experience when I say, "Go and find your authentic gifts and talents."

When I discovered my natural God-given abilities, I began cultivating ideas, planning, and seeking help from those who were already successful in doing what I wanted to accomplish. I took action by investing time and money in my education, and in seeking the services of people to help me acquire the wisdom, knowledge, and insight I needed to achieve my desired results, outcomes and experiences.

I learned early on in my journey to success to never compare my results to those of another individual. Every person's measurement for victory will and should always be different. When we start comparing and measuring our abilities and triumphs against someone else's apparent outcomes, it opens the door for fear to take residence in our heart. From the experience I'd been through in my childhood, I already knew that, by age eight, I had been introduced to fear, which caused me to lack confidence and doubt my abilities. The knowledge that this had been my story meant I had to learn to overcome the fear of failing by facing the giants of rejection, isolation, and gravely wounded feelings head-on. I had to learn to love myself all over again—to honor my boldness and courage. I could see how deeply ashamed I had been because of my parents' divorce. It was as if I suddenly had become part of lost or damaged goods. In my child's mind, I believed I had the best family and life. Anything less than that I refused to accept. The worry that my parents were not fighting hard enough to save their marriage and our family (in a little eight-year-old girl's mind) had set up fear, rejection, and defeat that plagued me for many years. I believed that, if my family could not win this battle, then surely, I would not have the strength, courage, or tenacity to overcome obstacles in my own life. It seemed inevitable that I would fail at anything I tried to accomplish.

And, for a long time, it looked that way. Every time a piercing or troublesome event would occur in my life, I refused to confront it. I always had to be the peacemaker. I guarded myself from anything or anyone who might cause me to feel like I was becoming a part of someone, or something, that would eventually be torn apart. The thought of being rejected or failing was always in my subconscious. Sadly, I was not aware of and did not recognize that this same vicious cycle was happening repeatedly until after I was married.

Subsequently, I began looking at behavior patterns; Man! They tell "perfect" stories when attention to detail is given. I could see clearly that I had never dealt with the issues of my childhood hurt and pain. Eventually, that same unchecked hurt and pain launched out to cause subtle (and some not so subtle) ripple effects in my life. Now I could at least attempt to loosen those tentacles that could have had devastating effects.

In the absolutely miraculous way that I had learned to recognize by following God's plan for me, I was able to turn fear on itself. To overcome my fear of failure, I made fear become afraid of attempting to approach me again. I made a conscious decision to look for who, what, when, where, why and how things evolved in my life without blaming anyone else for my poor decision-making as an adult. And to do that, I needed to understand the root causes of all my behavior—no matter how uncomfortable I became regarding what I found out.

Acquiring comprehensive knowledge, through gathering information and facts, as well as becoming skilled over time in grasping cause and effect (without blame), catapults us into greater wisdom, forgiveness, and grace. It teaches us how to evaluate experience from the proper perspective and not from a tunnel vision point of view. And more importantly, forgiving ourselves is extremely important in getting over fear. We only fail when we refuse to deal with unconscious patterns and behaviors from our past that lead to self-destruction. We can face our giants head on and live life to the fullest—free and victorious!

Today, as I consciously and honestly assess my effectiveness in my professional as well as personal life, I can say that my positive attitude and my ability to relate to people where they are both help to energize and refresh their lives daily. People want to see, feel, and know that there are others who believe in their dreams, ideas, and plans just as much as they do. The zeal I have to encourage someone to make better decisions that will cause them to be placed into better positions is paramount to my success in working with others. I learned firsthand that it is not enough to just say and think to ourselves, "I want better." Everyone needs someone to help them document what they see, create ideas, initiate proper planning, and measure outcomes, as well as gain invaluable awareness of understanding and embracing the process of life's obstacles while following their passion.

I had to learn to shift my way of thinking from being critical toward both myself and my experiences and to move forward in a positive direction. I think of it as "shifting the gears" in my head. Another analogy might be to use different qualities of fuel to get the best results from my (brain) engine. A car engine operates on a combustion system fueled by the grade of gas pumped into it (i.e., unleaded, plus, or premium). The grade of gas will determine the type of performance the car will have, but you must determine what it is you want, from minimum to maximum. Results can range from an extremely uncomfortable, bumpy ride all the way to a smooth one in which the bumps in the road are barely even noticeable. Practically speaking, the mind operates in the same manner. What we decide to feed into our mind determines what we become. In other words, people eventually become what they eat, drink, and think!

Subsequently, I needed to understand and acknowledge which areas of my life were impairing my mental capacity to succeed. I learned to question my thought process and patterns. I looked for answers and solutions for my own insecurities and negative thoughts. I incorporated praying and asking God for help, healing, and deliverance from anything hindering my growth and development from the largest to the smallest obstacle. Furthermore, I did not stop praying and asking questions until I received clear answers about my self-imposed familiar ceilings. Eventually, I realized that these answers had been inside of me all the time. At this point, my focus shifted to what I was capable of doing and was no longer stuck on what I could not accomplish. As I concentrated on my strengths and gradually worked on my weaknesses, I began to soar. I did not have time to worry about what was being left behind or potential roadblocks; I simply persisted in moving forward with excellence and pursuing my dreams.

Learning to believe in our dreams is critical to our personal success. We must first buy in to our own dreams and desires before anyone else will. More importantly, money cannot be the determining factor for following dreams. A wise person once told me to chase my passion, follow my dreams, and the money would come. Seems simple enough, doesn't it? But we must know how critical it is that our dream be our own and not what someone else would like us to achieve. As I explained earlier, we must recognize our natural gifts and talents. Not only must we recognize them, we must also know and understand the strengths and weaknesses of those gifts and talents and be willing to invest time and money toward sharpening our gifts and talents.

Finally, I want to state clearly that there is no such thing as reaching a pinnacle for learning and growing. We must continue to connect with others who are already achieving and excelling in our desired areas of interest and we should not ever be afraid of failing or making mistakes. They are inevitable and will happen; however, it is how we evaluate and learn from the mistakes and failures that will determine our altitude. We need to learn quickly, make adjustments, and not be afraid to think and do things "outside the box." I have found it essential to feed myself daily with scripture, to pray, to invest in my craft, to submit my plans to God, and to stay around positive people. It has also been vitally important and essential to me to find and cultivate a great support system. It may not be ready-made and waiting for every one of us, but we must not fret. We can look for like-minded individuals and connect with those we believe will help us to grow and succeed.

A dream will only come to life only when we take the action to set our goals, to grow, to develop, to invest time and money in ourselves, and to overcome our fears. We must never be afraid to strive for and be exceptional. Any one or all of us can begin living on our own terms...fully skilled in all the areas of our life.

"Don't be afraid of your own personal success. Own it and watch it multiply."

— *Dr. Nicoa Garrett*

Acknowledgments

To my husband (Larry Garrett), my number one fan and cheerleader. He speaks volumes of praise, wisdom and positive criticism into my life, which helps me to remain grounded, confident, and teachable. I thank him even more for consistently making me happy for 20 years, and many more to come. Thank you "Big Daddy" for allowing your flower to continuously bud and evolve into masterpieces, centerpieces, and sometimes, "crumb cake." When it seems like I just can't get it together, I always find a safe place to land inside your loving arms.

Thank you to my daughters, Alexis and Jalia for your support, unconditional love, and understanding. You are the absolute best children a mom could ask for. Great things are waiting for both of you. Go and make your impact on the world. Always allow the Lord to guide your steps. You two are truly amazing!

To my parents, George Wallace and Earleen Wallace, thank you for bringing me into the world. As a little girl, I always wanted to make both of you proud of me. In your own ways, both of you have helped me to become who I am today. I thank God for parents who support, encourage and, believe in me continuously. Mom and daddy, I love you!

To Dr. Kaye Smith, thank you for telling me with boldness that I had played it "too safe for too long." Those few words began to change my life almost immediately. Thank you for all the countless personal discussions, deep penetrating and thought-provoking meetings, concern for my family, standing by my side, prayers, and laughs. More importantly, I thank you for not being afraid to speak directly into my life when you thought something may need tweaking. You always knew how to teach, correct, build, and love. I love and miss you dearly!!

To my family, friends, and lovely *Destiny DeFined* Sisters, I say thank you with a grateful heart.

RADIANT

Dr. Phenessa A. Gray

Burn, Baby, Burn

"Some women fear the fire. Some women simply become it..."

— *R.H. Sin*

I never believed I was anyone special. Just a simple girl wanting a simple life—a white picket fence, a nice home, a doting husband, lots of babies, and to be the best stay-at-home pastor's wife possible so I could take care of my family. Well, I thought I wanted it. At least, this is the dream others wanted for me. Like all little girls, I grew up believing in fairy tales. Desperately fixated on Disney movies selling indoctrinated fantasies, I dreamed one day an adoring knight would pull me up on his black stallion and rescue me from my life into our happily ever after. Who wouldn't want adventure, suspense, and victory in the name of love, and of course, for God?

My life was anything but that. I grew up in the Southern Baptist tradition. We ate, breathed, and slept church rules and rituals. There were too many religious people telling me who I was, wasn't, or was supposed to be. It has taken my entire life so far to figure out who I was called to be. Who knew that I could dream, believe, and think for myself to create my own world? My story begins with trauma, but I believe it will end in triumph.

From the outside looking in, I realize I probably wasn't supposed to make it this far. As I think about what I've overcome, nothing but the grace of God has kept me sane and alive, even when I wanted to die. I often wondered why I felt so bad when, to those around me, it appeared that I had it all together? I learned very early to wear a mask to hide the pain and suffering within and around me. To others, my life seemed perfect. A master at appearances, I could perform effortlessly. After all, I had the best acting teachers—my church and my family. Television drama is supposed to be for entertainment, right? What happens when your life is the soap opera?

There's an old saying that states, "All that glitters is not gold." As I think back on my childhood, a myriad of emotions and thoughts floods my mind. Happiness and joy are not words I would use to describe it. It's not that I didn't have cheerful moments, but that's all they were—moments. Abuse was my norm. Yet, I didn't know what I experienced was abuse until much later in life. From a young age, I had been surviving life instead of living it. Unbeknownst to me, I was in the fire. The burning heat, although hurtful and painful, was too familiar. I learned to thrive in it. I lived in the fire to such a degree that when the heat wasn't on, everything felt out of place—like something was wrong. How warped my mind was!?! The battle to fight familiarity with dysfunction is a beast. The fire tests every facet of who you are. I've been good, I've been bad, and I've been ugly. What I have become in the process is nothing short of miraculous. Every moment of struggle or victory came together to make me who I am today. *RADIANT*.

As I recollect, I was in kindergarten when the first sexual abuse occurred. Unfortunately, it wouldn't be the last time. My babysitter used to put me in the closet and turn the lights off when she wanted to torture me, her friends wanted to smoke cigarettes, or her boyfriend showed up. She wasn't supposed to have those people at the house in the first place, but they would come over frequently. Needless to say, I spent a lot of time in the closet.

One evening while her boyfriend was there, she opened the closet door and told me to go into her bedroom. She began fondling me, saying that when I grew up, "this" is what a man would do to me. Her boyfriend agreed with her and began to touch my chest; I didn't have breasts yet. I remember feeling uncomfortable—nervous, strange, icky. I was warned that if I told anyone, I would not only get in trouble with my mother, but they would also whip me. This experience was the catalyst to so many other abuses that followed, as well as the repression of my emotions and my voice.

My babysitter and her boyfriend continued with this horrible behavior. Later, extended family members and a few kids at the bowling alley also began molesting me. Each time, either I was bullied into silence or my life was threatened if I didn't keep my mouth shut. I lived in constant fear that something bad would happen to me. I was warned my mother wouldn't love me anymore if I told. In my strict and religious family, we were taught to "be seen and not heard" and to "not ever air dirty laundry." I was also taught that my body was not my own and was created only for a man's pleasure. Eventually, I developed the ability to distance myself when bad things happened. Every instance of abuse triggered an out-of-body experience.

Because I was forced into silence, any kind of speaking became a huge fear of mine; it sometimes still is. I learned at an early age that I had no voice. I felt I had no one to share my heart with except God and my journal. This is how writing became my outlet and therapist. My journals became my voice.

My writing and my deep belief in God helped me survive the abuse, especially, what I experienced from one of my uncles. He constantly berated me when my mother wasn't around. She traveled for business often and trusted me into his care. Although he's quite different now, everyone was terrified of him then. I remember sometimes getting blamed or beaten when his children got into trouble. Everything seemed to be my fault. I was told that I would "never amount to anything," called names like "spoiled brat," "fast," "stupid," "retarded," and also told, "All you're ever gonna be is a hooker on a street corner." I felt like a mistake—like I could never do anything right.

To add insult to injury, my father and mother divorced when I was an infant, so my uncle was my main male role model. I had no concept of what a father was or how to relate to men. I saw glimpses of fatherhood with my other uncles and their children; nevertheless, I felt disconnected. All I had of my biological father were a few tattered photos my mom kept in an old family album. I used to stare at those pictures for hours. I didn't know him, but I fiercely wanted him in my life. This desperate need fueled my quest to try to find him. I foolishly thought he would rescue me from this hell—kind of like that knight on the black stallion. I was wrong. My mom reluctantly gave me my paternal grandmother's phone number, so I could find him. My mother wanted to protect me from my father, although I didn't know why. Eventually, I found out. When we spoke, it was like talking to a stranger and unpleasant. He reinforced the negative words my uncle told me. One of the worst conversations entailed him casually telling me that I was "a waste of flesh and bone." Later, he wrote my mother a letter telling her he wanted nothing to do with me. This experience, along with my uncle's view of me, shaped my perception of who I was...nothing. It also shaped my expectations of and treatment by men. Raised to respect my elders and the man as the head of the household, I succumbed to a subservient role in relationships and repressed any feelings to speak up. What was my voice going to do anyway but make matters worse? Covertly, I was becoming a quiet, seething, perfect storm.

I struggled in school because of these horrible, early childhood experiences. A defining moment in my childhood was when I found out my second-grade teacher, Mrs. Brown, assumed I would always struggle intellectually. She said, "I hope you grow up to be beautiful and marry rich because you'll never make it past high school." Ignoring this negative teacher's behavior, my mother was determined that I would learn by any means necessary. Learning became a painful process with my ABC's beaten into me. I had a speech impediment and, if that wasn't bad enough, additional testing revealed that I had dyslexia.

Later in life, further tests showed that I also had central auditory processing disorder and post-traumatic stress disorder (PTSD). To help me deal with these challenges, my mother removed me from public school and enrolled me into private school with better, individualized instruction. In the afternoon and on the weekends, I went to a school for students with special needs. I learned study strategies and coping mechanisms that ultimately became innate. Overall, learning became easier; however, new hurdles arose personally and socially. I had an action plan for learning, but not for living.

My home life was still hellacious. I was anxious and jumpy all the time. Feelings of stupidity, not being good enough, worthlessness, and being unloved continued to haunt me. Trusting others and myself was extremely difficult. I hated my life and I hated myself. I thought about suicide regularly, but the fear of going to hell for taking my life superseded the pain of living. After all, religion teaches that "real" Christians do not kill themselves; they trust in the Lord. As time went on, I became numb to the pain and merely existed.

As I got older, my childhood experiences continued to influence all of my relationships. College was a nightmare of trying to fit in and failing every time. I was so young and naïve. The rage inside me manifested when a group of girls tried to jump me after a fraternity party. I was sick and tired of the bullying and the name-calling of people taking my kindness for weakness. The docile, quiet church girl became a raging fire.

From then on, I went from one extreme to the other; balance was non-existent, but I didn't know any better. My life flipped upside down, especially after my grandmother died in 1993. I started binge drinking, wild partying and fighting. I began living recklessly. This Southern Baptist church girl became hell on earth. I got into numerous abusive relationships (emotional, psychological, sexual, spiritual, and physical). On separate occasions, several previous boyfriends, a police officer, and two guys I barely knew raped me. It happened so often I believed it was normal. One rape resulted in pregnancy, but, God, like he so often does, turned this potential tragedy into a blessing—my daughter is a miracle in my life.

In retrospect, I don't remember a time as I was growing up when I wasn't abused in some way. This added to my feelings of worthlessness. I felt like garbage, and the people around me made sure I continued to feel this way. Every time I was abused, I either considered or attempted suicide.

In 2004, this vicious cycle became "darkest just before the dawn." A counselor, who was also an elder at church, violated my trust in a humiliating way. After all I had been through, that was the absolute worst. I'd never thought I needed protection from someone at church. My mom told me that even the church has demons, but I never believed her until then. This same elder later became a pastor.

After this, I was confused, lost and utterly cast down—having the most heinous, diabolical experience a believer could imagine. The earlier abuses seemed to pale in comparison. It's almost impossible to recover from any sexual abuse; however, when it feels like your very soul has been raped, the wounds and scars are deep and often neverending. All I had was God! This last violation of me threatened everything I thought I knew about Him. I almost lost my mind.

For several years, the battle for control of my mind began with consistent, methodical brainwashing and manipulation in the guise of counseling sessions. Numerous times, I tried to leave him and the church. He would threaten to kill himself if I did. There were times when I would hear his gun clicking in the background while we were on the phone. Click. Click. Click. My heart would race. He said that his blood would be on my hands, and I'd never please God or be blessed if I left him. He asked me to marry him several times; he said that we were eternally connected and I would not be who I was supposed to be in God without him in my life. I was so scared; I submitted to staying and did whatever he asked of me.

Depressed and exhausted, I suffered from panic attacks and insomnia. I had very little sleep helping him build his church over a five-month span. I felt so trapped. I prayed for God to deliver me. One night, I took matters into my own hands to stop my feelings of hopelessness, helplessness, and intense pain. I swallowed a lot of pills and woke up three days later in the Intensive Care Unit on a respirator. With tubes protruding from my body, I couldn't move. I couldn't speak. I couldn't even breathe on my own. All I could do was think. I can't tell you how many pills were in those bottles, but I will tell you how grateful and glad I am that God spared my life. I asked Him to help me and promised that if He could get me out of this, I would never try to kill myself again.

Still, my world was falling apart. I had lost much more than my voice and my ability to move. I had lost whatever was left of myself. And, worse yet, I thought I had lost my salvation. I mean, how could God forgive me for being so stupid? I was surely going to hell in a fiery hand basket. The truth is, God spared me for a reason. I began the search to find out why. I reached out to various ministries such as The Hope of Survivors and therapists to help me find my way through the healing process. It wasn't easy. Many times, I wanted to quit and give up again on life. What kept me going was the promise I made to God in the hospital, though I did have moments when keeping that promise was very hard.

But I'm still here! And yes, I still struggle. Eventually, I did move on, but not without a cost. I've been homeless several times, and have lost all my possessions, but I never lost God. Even when I thought I did, He was always near. He truly is *"close to the brokenhearted and saves those who are crushed in spirit"* (Psalm 34:18, New International Version). I've been truly blessed in my life's journey, but it hasn't been without trouble. At that time however, I hadn't received the revelation that no one's life is devoid of trouble. Since then, I've learned to look within to discover my gifts and strengths in order to overcome struggles. Ironically, the one perceived weakness I had as a child became a great strength.

I was able to use school as a coping mechanism to get through my heartaches and hardships. I furthered my education to get my mind off my inner turmoil. The little girl hearing her second-grade teacher say she wouldn't make it past high school is now a grown woman with five academic degrees and several certifications!

Looking back, the choice to pursue my doctorate was such an easy decision, but the journey to that end became a huge obstacle. I can truly say, from personal experience, that anyone who graduates with a doctorate must have an unparalleled stick-to-it-iveness mentality. Like a phoenix, we rise from the ashes of our former selves, environments, and experiences into a renewed, resolute being. I can attest that this happened to me.

I must admit I was afraid. At the time, I had a seven-year-old daughter, a new baby girl, and an unsupportive husband—as if I needed anything else to occupy my time. Yet, I knew if I didn't pursue my doctorate then, I probably never would. I already regretted many things in my life. I didn't want procrastination to be another deterrent. Meanwhile, those "not good enough" voices still filled my head. Can I really do this? Is it the right time? Should I do this right now while dealing with body shame after gaining 110 pounds from a high-risk pregnancy, postpartum depression, financial troubles, and a failing marriage with a person who didn't want to touch me anymore? I was still wondering, "Why is this my life?" I was completely overwhelmed, but I also wanted to go back to school! It's crazy, right?

Being the risk-taker I had become, I jumped into the academic fire. Through divorce, bouts of unemployment, and even periods of homelessness,

I continued to pursue my degree. It appeared to be the only constant in my life. Still needing to heal, one could say I "self-medicated" with school. Unconsciously, I had something to prove. I needed to prove I am good enough. I am smart enough. I am capable enough. I am more than my looks. I am more than my past. I am more than my mistakes. I. AM. ENOUGH. I. AM. MORE.

Comically, school kept me sane, except for the times I thought it would drive me insane. I remember a life-changing moment toward the end of my academic efforts. For the life of me, I could not connect the themes in my qualitative study. My living room looked like a post-it notes explosion—a carpet of many colors. Themes were color-coded in piles upon piles of fluorescent paper. I thought I was doing well until suddenly I felt overwhelmed. My heart started to beat out of my chest. My palms were sweaty. Thoughts of, "Why am I doing this?" and "I can't do this!" bombarded my mind. I became that little girl in the closet again, feeling alone, trapped, and scared. There I was, a full-time, single mother, a full-time employee, a full-time student, and on the floor about to have a full-time nervous breakdown. I was so disappointed in myself. My dissertation was on emotional intelligence, and I was sitting on the floor sobbing, snotting, and an emotional wreck! Had I not learned anything? In exasperation, I called my dissertation mentor, and she slowly pulled me off the figurative ledge. She told me that my feelings were normal and that I needed to take a break. A break? I honestly could not remember how to take a break. With the pressures of the quarter ending, I had maxed out my student loans to the point I could not get any more funding. I had to complete my dissertation this quarter, so a break sounded like nonsense to me. But I took her advice, and I'm glad I did. After that, everything fell into place. Even with all the fiery trials and tribulations, I earned the highest academic degree in April of 2017.

I thought I would be on cloud nine; however, all those repressed emotions and feelings came up all at once. Then, as people around me started learning of my accomplishment, their masks began to crack. I began to see which ones were for me and which ones were against me. I found out, however, that not everyone shared my excitement. Some who started on the journey with me recognized the difference in me. Others couldn't handle the change and resisted it. Truly, I was a different person. In my mind, it was for the better. Change in a person can become a mirror to another. The reflection of what one should do, or could do, or could be, can require too much. People near you face the risky challenge of holding on to their excuses as to why they haven't accomplished their own dreams. So, guess what happens? They begin to belittle your dreams. I lost two marriages while working on my doctorate, but I also lost my former self, my valuing of others' (friends and family included) expectations of me, and my relentless need to please others despite dying inside myself. Yes, I lost much, but I gained so much more.

I gained myself. Through this journey, I rescued the little girl who was told many years ago to "be seen and not heard." She wasn't meant to just be seen; she also had to be heard. My courage and strength grew in this refining process. Then, I was able to give the little girl in me a platform to speak her truth. I gave her back her voice. Now, I wanted to help others rescue their voices. Through my own struggles to express my emotions and open my mouth, I found my purpose and passion.

My younger self is still within me. The moments I feel like a child again, I tell myself, "Don't doubt who you are. You are valued and invaluable. You are more than enough. Your voice matters. You are loved." I needed to hear those words when I was younger. I still need to hear those words today.

I never set out to be anyone's shero. Mostly, I was trying to rescue myself! In 2008, my life's calling was reignited. I founded Bodacious Women, a women's group of professionals, who gathered to talk about what we couldn't share in boardrooms, classrooms, churches, workplaces, and our homes. We could share what dwelt inside of us without fear of judgment or punishment. We could break bread together and laugh, cry, and heal.

My dreams have experienced numerous iterations because I've experienced numerous iterations. For so long, I felt unworthy, undervalued, and unloved. I've suffered from depression, insomnia, and even suicidal thoughts—all by-products of PTSD. I've dealt with being labeled crazy. And even though society may tell me otherwise, and the world sometimes seems to be crashing in on me, I know that I am here for a purpose. I've had to go through the process of acknowledging, identifying, and managing my emotions too many times to count. One thing I am certain of, and that has stood the test of time, is God. He is my constant. He is always my foundation to fall back on and my reason for living this life.

Society will usually label what it doesn't understand. I've embraced being misunderstood and I welcome those who experience the same. Most creatives, highly sensitive persons (HSP), and empaths are very special people—probably more so because they are misunderstood. We can see and feel what others can't and can therefore provide unique solutions to real-world problems. But, we must embrace what makes us different and to successfully use this intuitive gift. We can't be afraid to stand out from the crowd.

Regardless of the evolving forms of my organization, the mission and passion remain the same—to empower others no matter who they are or their stage in life. I think of myself as a Soul-Whisperer/Soul-Surgeon. I want to give voice to people's truth. I expose hidden beliefs, thoughts, attitudes, and emotions. Then, I can empower authenticity and creativity. But, as I have explained, first, I have to do this with myself. Reinventing myself will be a continuous, lifelong endeavor. I'll never remain the same. I'm always learning and changing into a better version of myself. Because

I've personally experienced this, I can use this powHer to help and empower others. I don't discriminate. Each of us has a superpower to unleash. I desire to assist in the unleashing process through the gifts and talents God's given me to help others share what God's given them.

The doctoral journey honed my passion for authenticity and creativity. The ability to truly embrace both our truth and The Truth, is freeing. When we're able to attain this freedom, the sky is not the limit—it's only the beginning. God's universe opens doors for us, and our own creativity is birthed. Because we are created beings, the very essence of what made us is in us. We become creators, and therein lies my passion. This is my *Destiny DeFined*—to empower others to be and live their truth on their journey to finding The Truth. I've had to travel this "road less traveled" myself and understand the emerging emotions from beginning to end.

My life's purpose is to help others feel better, think better, and create their better world through creative exploration. I desire to strengthen community with art and soul. The main problem I am focused on is society's incessant need to mask truth.

Passion and success are synonymous to me. My Truth is my motivation; my passion is my success. Acceptance of your truth is the bravest thing you can do. Your truth challenges the status quo. Your truth turns the tides and leaves a ripple effect in the ocean of life. Your truth, should you choose to accept it, is a game changer. Your truth is the fire-starter. Matthew 5:14-16 (English Standard Version) says, "*You are the light of the world. A city set on a hill cannot be hidden. Nor do people light a lamp and put it under a basket, but on a stand, and it gives light to all in the house. In the same way, let your light shine before others, so that they may see your good works and give glory to your Father who is in heaven.*" In essence, YOU are the light. We all were created to be radiant. The Oxford Pocket English Dictionary defines radiant as "sending out light; shining or glowing brightly; (of a person or their expression) clearly emanating great joy, love, or health; and, (of an emotion or quality) emanating powerfully from someone or something; very intense or conspicuous." God created us to be His Light and we must intentionally *"...walk as children of light (for the fruit of light is found in all that is good and right and true)"* (Ephesians 5:8-9, ESV). My advice to you to practice being radiant is to stay lit no matter what comes your way. How do you stay lit? One word: PURSUE. Pursue your idea or dream with reckless abandon. Don't stop until you see the dream the way it's etched in your mind come to fruition. Many people will not understand or support your vision. This is all a part of the journey. If we are living, we should be learning and evolving. We are always becoming. Don't be afraid to become who you were always meant to be. Don't fear the fire around you. Let the fire around you ignite the radiant fire within you and blaze new trails with your trials.

I stopped running from the fire and became the fire. I stopped allowing others to tell me who I am or am not. I stopped begging for a seat at everyone else's tables and allowing them to douse my fire. I decided I was powerful beyond measure to create my own table. Now, I have an urgency to light the dwindling or non-existent flames of others to be all they can be. The world needs people like me. The world needs people like you. The world is waiting. So, let's get lit together!

As I close, allow me to leave you with this thought. In everything, we must consider the tangible and intangible costs. What are you willing to give up or sacrifice to discover who you are? For your dream? For you? Unfortunately, those who started with you may not finish the race with you. This too is all a part of the journey. This journey includes checks and balances and losses and gains. We are processed through our process. We are refined by the fire to one day become our own fire. We discover our authentic selves and that's a crazy, beautiful experience, but well worth it. All it takes is a choice. Are you ready for your truth? Are you ready to be a light? What will you choose today? I have become my fire. I pray you choose you and let yourself become your fire as well. My friends, become radiant. Stay lit and burn, baby, burn!

Acknowledgments

"And I will bring the third part through the fire, Refine them as silver is refined, And test them as gold is tested They will call on My name, And I will answer them; I will say, 'They are My people,' And they will say, 'The LORD is my God'" (Zechariah 13:8-9, New American Standard).

First and foremost, I dedicate my chapter and journey to my Lord and Savior, Jesus Christ, for which I could not have accomplished this without Him. I am immensely thankful to my first role model and mother, Carlond Gray, who raised me as a single mother while maintaining full-time and part-time jobs and obtaining four academic degrees, among many other accomplishments. She is the epitome of resilience and it runs through our veins. I am thankful for my awesome daughters, Hannah and Trinity, who empower and motivate me every day to keep pressing forward and made me laugh when I wanted to cry. You are truly my angels sent from God. I am thankful to the other queens of *Destiny DeFined* for being more than a group of exemplary women, but sisters who love, trust, and undergird each other no matter what comes our way. Thank you to my mentor, Dr. Patricia Parham, classmates, colleagues, and friends who provided daily encouragement, support, and guidance to help me progress through my doctoral journey and my life.

Lastly, thank you to every adversity, failure, missed opportunity, trial, tribulation, loss, and pain. I've been refined and tested by fire, have came forth as pure gold, and I don't even smell like smoke! Adversity, you pushed me closer to God. Now, I have an amazing relationship with my Abba Father, who taught me how to depend solely on Him, rest in His Love and Strength, rise, shine, and burn for the cause of Christ to advance His Kingdom. Thank you, Pappa!

RECREATE

Angela Malone

Chapter 5

Transform and Break Free

"My mission in life is not merely to survive, but to thrive; and to do so with some passion, some compassion, some humor, and some style."

— *Maya Angelou*

There are a number of things I do not enjoy doing. I guess, in that way, I might be like a lot of people. But here I am, one of the authors of this book, when the truth is: I seriously don't like talking (or writing) about myself! In therapy, I often express to my clients that "healing begins when you step outside of your comfort zone." Brene Brown states "Vulnerability is basically uncertainty, risk, and emotional exposure." Well, I like comfort because it is safe and secure. But I'm going to practice what I've been preaching, with the help and strong support of my fabulous sisters and fellow authors of our book. I'm going to allow myself to be vulnerable in order to offer hope and strength to our readers, as well as to encourage those who want to pursue a higher education, become an entrepreneur, or both. I also want to speak to a large number of individuals who can't yet put their finger on "what they want to be when they grow up." I invite you to come along with me, as I step out of my own comfort zone and share my story.

Who I Was

From an early age, I have used events and circumstances in my life as motivational strategies for advancement. Growing up in the small town of New Madrid, MO, opportunities were limited, especially for the African-American community. I'm not going to write a full autobiography, but I do want to share the "backstory" so that my readers can see what I know from experience. And that is: It does not matter how, when, or where you begin your life journey; it matters how you continue it. My life has been very instrumental in my education and career advancement.

I'm the middle child of five siblings, and I lived my childhood as the "spoiled" girl. Yes, I know they say the middle child is usually overlooked, but not in my case. My parents always said, "I was free-spirited and stubborn." I still carry these traits today, and they can sometimes be both positive and negative attributes. I spent a long time focusing on the positive, because who wants to address anything negative—things that make us feel pain, regret, or shame? As I've gotten older, however, I've realized that the willingness to explore areas of hurt in our lives is necessary. I'll expound on that later.

When I was ten, my life transitioned from a place of happiness and enjoyment to a period of hurt, sadness, disappointment, hate, and revenge. I lost one of my favorite aunts. I loved my auntie; she was so pretty, and I loved her smile, which could light up a room. This loss was my first true heartache. I recall asking myself so many questions: Why did this happen? What could I have done to prevent it? Why didn't anyone stop it? Why didn't my grandmother, grandfather, dad, aunties, and uncles do something to help her? I couldn't understand why nobody did anything to change what happened. These questions tore at me for many years afterward.

Her death impacted my life so deeply and influenced me in so many different ways, but I suppressed the emotions surrounding it for many years. At the age of eleven, I made a life goal of going to law school and opening up my aunt's case because, although her death was investigated, no one was ever arrested or convicted of her murder. I kept most of my pain secret from my parents and anyone else around me. I vowed repeatedly to myself that I was not going to end up like my aunt. These pledges meant not trusting a man at all: if he was not my daddy or my brothers, always be in control; never date longer than three months (no need to get attached); and, to find the person or persons responsible for my aunt's death. For the next twenty years, I was on a search to find justice. In some of my searching, I found comfort, and other times just more pain and agony.

I was working on my undergraduate degree when I found out the statute of limitation for murder had not run out, and I called my dad. I was excited because it meant there was a light at the end of the tunnel. I thought my dad would give me the go ahead, but he didn't. I was stopped by, "Angela, leave that alone." However, my question of why he hadn't done anything got answered. His response was, "I wanted to kill him, but I thought about your mother, you and your brothers and sister. It would have been unfair for you all not to be with your father." He also shed light on why they didn't help my auntie before it happened. My father let me know they tried numerous times to help, but she refused to listen, and there was no more they could do. His response provided me a level of understanding, but I still wanted justice. I hated the person I felt was responsible for my aunt's death and had literally gotten away with murder.

I had been taught not to hate, but I hated him with every fiber of my being, and it bled over into several areas of my life. If you ask any of my college friends about me, they would all say I was mean. All of my rage was projected onto other people. Although I was hurting, I didn't want other people to see it, and the hurt defined my life for a long time.

I decided my pain would be my motivation and would help me for the rest of my life; let's just say there's a difference in the child mind and the adult mind. In 2004, God really showed me that He was in control, and I would have to process my hurt. I didn't realize I would have to go through my own transformation to obtain the goals I desired. This is the beginning of addressing my core issues and really coming to understand what it meant to be vulnerable.

A Mid-Life Crisis, Already

At the age of 25, I had the kind of life crisis many people don't experience until they're close to fifty. I had my life all planned out: what I was going to do, where I was going to live, how much money I would make, and when I was going to be married. All of those plans you make when you THINK you are in control of your own destiny. I had completed my bachelor's degree, was completing my first master's degree and preparing to attend law school. (Remember my promise to myself when I was a young girl? That I would make a case against my aunt's killer and see that she got justice!) I was also a single mother of a four-year-old. Although, she is one of the greatest miracles of my life, having a child before I graduated with my bachelor's degree was not in my original plan. So, I had to get things done and done right, because I had another mouth to feed. I had just moved to Florida from Missouri and was ready to start law school in 2005. I knew what I wanted, but I never stopped to think about what God might want for me. Suddenly, it seemed as if out of the blue, I began getting a vision of a building (Remember, I said I was stubborn, and this was when that stubbornness manifested in my life the most). I didn't try to determine what the vision was about or if maybe it was some sort of sign about my future. I didn't create it, so it couldn't be that important. Well, I was not going to let anyone control my life, not even God.

For sure, the vision troubled me, but I kept telling myself that I knew all the necessary things I had to do. I told myself it probably didn't mean anything and would fade away in time. I was mistaken and the vision became stronger and appeared more frequently. Eventually, I found myself talking to God, saying, "God, I don't know what you are doing or trying to tell me, but I'm going to law school."

I was at work one day—I remember it was raining—and the vision appeared again. Crying, I called my best friend's father, who was a pastor, and told him what was happening. I said I didn't know what to make of it, and that I was tired of having it. Of course, I now know that calling him was really about him telling me what the vision meant. I can still hear him saying, "God is trying to show you something, but he is not ready to reveal it all because you are not ready for it." I argued with him. "No, I don't think this is meant for me because I know what I want to do." I remember him laughing and saying what I wanted didn't matter; it was what God wanted. Feeling more resistant and disbelieving than ever, I laughed at the idea. Why not? After all, just moments before that, I had been crying. My emotions were clearly volatile. So much for me being in control of everything. One of the downsides of my stubbornness is that it created cycles of depression, confusion, inconsistencies, the inability to receive and accept feedback, and at times the fear that my life was just a lie. If I had a dollar for every time someone told me, "Angela you don't listen," I would be a millionaire.

The turning point came over a year later, after I had been working with the mental health/substance abuse population. On a rainy day, I was sitting in my car and for some reason my heart was very full, but not with despair. A change had come over me that I could feel, even though it was hard to put it into the right words. I called my dad. I said, "I don't think I'm supposed to be a lawyer; I believe God is pulling me to help people." My dad's answer was, "What we want to do is not always what God wants us to do. You have to allow God to lead you." I remembered having heard these same words a year before and laughing at them, but this time, I was receptive. I certainly didn't have my life, or even myself, together, but now I might find a direction. I began to take what was going on inside me seriously. One of the best things I ever did was to seek out therapy. It was challenging and tough, but rewarding. I went in with the position that I was closed and willing to share only a little if I had to.

One of the many questions I remember my therapist asking was, "When are you going to get off the roller coaster?" In my mind, what she was calling the roller coaster was actually a safe place, no matter how up and down it was. I thought I was in control of all the changes that came along. Reality hit me when I discovered, through counseling, that I was operating in fear. I was afraid to relinquish control and become vulnerable with myself and others. But when I did, I was able to cry and release all those years of anger, hatred, and resentment. As I endured this process, it became clear that God had been giving me the vision, and from being simply a repeated vision of a building, it grew into the foundation for the wonderful business I still have today: Innovation Counseling Center. Innovation Counseling Center is a practice where individuals can come to start on their healing journey. Individuals can come and learn to transform their lives and break free from their bondages. I now understand my passion to lead, train, transform, and empower others and feel I know why God has always led me on my life and educational journey.

I Will Be Dr. Malone

I guess I am my own obstacle and my own distraction. And there have been so many times I just wanted to say, "I'm done." At those moments, I've looked into my daughter's face and remembered how I have empowered her whenever she had difficulties in school and dance. I thank God for my family and friends who have talked me off the ledge when I wanted to give up. Still today, they're pulling for me as I finish up my dissertation, because, like me, they believe I will be Dr. Malone.

When I complete my doctorate, I will be done with school. I suspect many of my family members and friends do not believe me, because they have already identified me as "the life-time student." They're right! I will continue to learn— but not by getting another degree. The achievement of my doctoral degree will be very rewarding, but as soon as possible after that, I really do want my life back.

I was more than nervous starting the doctoral program. I was working full-time, was also a full-time mother, and had already started my business. But, as trying as it was, I wouldn't change my experience in my program one bit. I remember that first day, walking into my first class, and seeing women students who looked like me, Black women who had dreams and a passion to be more than the status quo. We created a bond that felt like a true sisterhood. Without it, I wonder how I would have made it this far in the program. It was more than great to have a support group in which I could vent—talk about confusing assignments, share my daily struggles, and express my frustration with online classmates that hit my last nerve.

I still have my sisters who were with me from the beginning, and even some new ones who have joined with us because of the deep bond we share. We are a group of Black women who encourage each other every day to press forward—to "lean in" to succeed. We are shattering the centuries-old stigmas attached to Black women. We continue to bring forth the new story of who we are and who we can be in this American society.

Our wise sister and hero, Angela Davis, talked about this journey so beautifully:

> "Black women have had to develop a larger vision of our society than perhaps any other group. They have had to understand white men, white women, and black men. And they have had to understand themselves. When black women win victories, it is a boost for virtually every segment of society."

I am so blessed and privileged to be affiliated with women who have experienced racism, discrimination, and injustices, but who remain willing to face these obstacles and not be deterred from pursuing their dreams and aspirations.

My Motivation

Fear paralyzed me for so much of my younger life. Fear of loss of control, fear that I was not enough, and yes, even fear of success. I used to think the latter couldn't ever be an issue for me, because I was focused on success no matter what—even at the cost of closing myself off to God's plan for me. So why would I be afraid to succeed? Because of the responsibility to "keep it up." And because of how much others would expect of me once I was a success.

Thankfully, I have learned the importance of seeking God first in everything in my life, and in doing that, coming to know who I really am. Often times we forget who we are because of our hurt and pain, and we lose sight of the beautiful flower we are. And often times we stop caring for ourselves and begin the process of killing ourselves—either quickly or slowly. We forget how much love and beauty we hold and allow one pain after another to define our presence in the world. We have to remember the beauty that is rooted inside of us. We have to nurture and groom ourselves in order for the growth process to take place. In this nurturing and grooming process, the issues we have suppressed will rise up and make themselves clear. Then we can process them in the best way and begin healing. The process will bring freedom, clarity, increase emotional regulation, and the ability to build healthy relationships.

I've finally learned that the real key to success is my willingness to endure the inevitable failures along the way. I have failed as a daughter, sister, mother, student, and business owner. In essence, as one of God's creations. In these most recent ones, I've learned so much from my mistakes. If we don't make mistakes, we don't allow for teachable moments and growth. Psalm 34:19 (King James Version) states, "*Many are the afflictions of the righteous: but the LORD delivereth him out of them all.*"

My journey, although it started a number of years ago, when I was small and using my own ideas to "stomp" my way to adulthood, has really just gotten on track. I now know that there is a path of true value ahead, although I can't always see the details of what it will include. I am so elated to see what is entailed. I need to continue to trust God for guidance, strength, and the ability to endure, even in those moments when I don't understand any of it.

What has helped me tremendously is writing out my vision and making it into a formal plan. It is necessary to write out your vision and make it plain. I like the way John Maxwell states that it takes a clear vision to create a masterpiece. I have found the importance of knowing my "Why Factor"— my passion—to create and *Recreate* the clearest vision possible. I used to keep things to myself, but I've learned that sharing my ideas with others, especially mentors, is essential to refining my vision.

I've also learned to use any and all of my resources. This has included reading a number of books on counseling and leadership. They offer me great guidance and direction. I've actively sought help from mentors in different stages of my life journey to help direct me and provide me necessary feedback. But, I always have to remind myself that they are not going to tell me simply what I want to hear. Sometimes, their feedback will be flat out uncomfortable; but I have to be ready if I'm going to actually progress.

To those of you who have been patient enough to read my story and consider my thoughts on how I came to have the gratitude in which I now live, I have one more thing to add: Don't give up, wherever you are on your path. And don't be afraid to follow your dreams and do it your way.

Acknowledgments

First, I would like to thank God for giving me the strength and knowledge to endure to the end. I would like to thank my parents, Nathaniel and Alecia Malone, for always encouraging and pushing me even when I wanted to give up. Thank you for allowing me to be myself and not trying to quiet me, even when I wasn't politically correct.

To my baby girl, Zariah Malone, it amazes me that you are about to embark on your own life journey. Just remember to always do it "your" way. Since you entered into this world, you have been my motivation. I have been in school since your conception and I'm glad you have been able to see the struggle and tears I have endured to make it to the end. Just know I will always love you "to the moon and back."

Julian Smalls, thank you for the years of friendship and companionship you have given me. You have heard my complaints, frustrations, and happy moments. You continue to tell me of my potential and my need to embrace it. Thank you for being you. Thank you to my siblings, Nathaniel, Yolanda, Nathan, Terrance, and Michael and my bestie/sister, Faith: Just know you all rock and are the best. To my special cousin-sister, Zianna Buchanan, thank you. Thank you to all my BBB sisters and my sisters of *Destiny DeFined* because we did it "*R*" way and we "*R*" winning.

RESTORATION
Dr. J. Sabrina Simmons

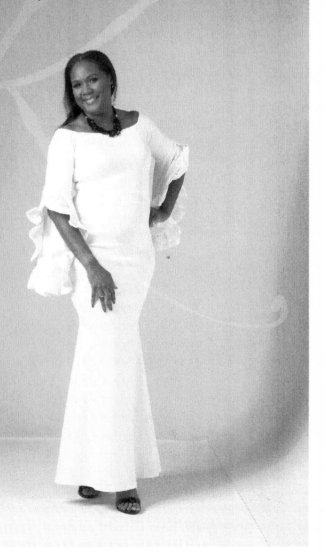

Never Give Up~Press Forward!

"The future belongs to those who believe in the beauty of their dreams."

— Eleanor Roosevelt

I dedicate this to my beloved father, Tenny Rudolph Smith, Sr.

It was Memorial Day weekend. I was sitting at my home away from home, Panera Bread, eating and working feverishly to complete my dissertation—dotting the last 'I' and crossing the last 'T.' This was indeed a crucible moment in my journey to becoming Dr. J. Sabrina Simmons.

Let me go back in time and share how it all started. Everyone's path to receiving a doctoral degree is different. For me, it began on a beautiful hot summer day. I begin to pray and ask for direction for my next life assignment. About thirty days later, I received a confirmation to start doing research on doctoral programs. After going through the process of elimination, I met with a friend, who has been instrumental in my educational life and professional career over the years. Ten minutes into our conversation, he said, "Sabrina, you will need a couple of letters of recommendation to start school, and I will write the first letter for you." I quickly picked up the phone and called my executive mentor, who was then my best friend and business partner. Without hesitating, they both agreed to write letters. In less than an hour, I was enrolled in Nova Southeastern University's Doctoral Program. WOW! It was clearly evident that starting a doctoral program was my next assignment. Also, professionally, I believed this was the right decision at the right time. I became truly excited about the opportunities, possibilities, and open doors a doctoral degree would provide for the women I was inspiring, coaching, and mentoring—and certainly for my family.

As I think back on that beautiful day at that favorite eating place—now my study hall as well, and I remember so vividly the moment I pressed the ENTER key to send my final draft to the dissertation chair; I could finally see the light at the end of the tunnel. I picked up my cell phone and dialed my dissertation chair. "Hello, Doctor, please check your email. My dissertation is complete, ready for review, and in your inbox!" I could tell she was pleased and went right to her computer to read my dissertation.

Concern was just around the corner. She couldn't get it open! I spent the next thirty minutes trying to stay calm as I would send, try different versions, and resend; however, nothing worked. The document was not openable! And I was not alone in starting to get uncomfortable. The worst-case scenario seemed to be shared between us. We both knew how critical it was for her to review the document and provide feedback because the deadline for me to take part in the commencement ceremony was at hand. I needed to have my dissertation submitted and reviewed by both chairs within the week to receive participation approval. It would be an understatement to say that the pressure was intense!

Unfortunately, after multiple tries, she still could not access the document. I felt sucker-punched. My heart seemed to drop into the pit of my stomach. And, sure enough, two days later, I received the final call from my wonderful chair notifying me I was not going to be able to participate in this year's commencement ceremony. I felt an ocean of emotions, and I felt overwhelmed for the second time. Up until this point, everything had gone exceptionally well during the entire doctoral program. Yes, I had a couple of bumps here and there, but nothing to bring me to tears; however, on this day I cried like a newborn baby.

I was meeting with a friend when I received their final decision. As I put my cell phone down, I felt numb. My friend said, "What's wrong?" The words fell slowly from my mouth, and hot tears ran down my cheeks as I said, "I'm not going to participate in this year's commencement ceremony." Of course, my friend was very empathetic and supportive.

Within minutes of that unhappy event, the Holy Spirit reminded me: "*And we know that all things work together for good to them that love God, to them who are called according to his purpose*" (Romans 8:28, King James Version). Yes, I love the Lord, so I knew somehow this situation had to work for my good. I remember saying out loud, "Lord, you did not commission me to go through this program to throw in the towel." At that moment, I knew giving up was not an option. We began to contact advisors and leaders to see if there were any exceptions to the commencement deadline rule—since I had in fact, submitted my document within the final deadline timeframe. After speaking with both the dean of education and the student union leader, it was determined that they could not change the policy for just one person.

I had to face facts. Life happens to everyone! And sometimes things are out of our control. I had received the news about the graduation ceremony, which did not seem good for me. My beautiful chair had done the best she could with the tools she was given. We had both been unable to change the rules. Now, I needed to process the impact of this news. I asked myself, "What's the worst thing that could happen?" My dissertation would be submitted and approved two or three weeks later than expected and I would still be able to participate in the following year's commencement program.

Whenever I receive disappointing news, I turn to the enlightening, unadulterated Word of God to align my perspective, realign my expectations, and transform my thoughts. The Word of God, praise, and comfort from the Holy Spirit always ignites my faith and renews my mind.

I obtained wonderful lessons learned throughout the years from my cousin and spiritual dad. The mentoring, encouragement, and spiritual development I received from him for over 20 years assisted me tremendously during this process. This moment in my education journey created the perfect recipe, and yes, an opportunity to apply the aforementioned spiritual and natural principles to never give up and press forward in this journey. I clearly understood I was already victorious. I encouraged myself with prayer, the word of God, fasting, and praise. Additionally, my personal prayer partners and my close friends consistently interceded throughout this educational journey for me. Yes, my perspective about the situation changed and everything was working together for my good because I love the Lord; I believe and apply His word. He has always been faithful, and I was confident the Lord would carry me through this test.

My dissertation was completed three weeks later. I was officially conferred as Dr. J. Sabrina Simmons. And, as a result of what happened, an email communication was created and sent from the Dean of Education's Office to all doctoral students advising them of critical dates and relevant information. Perhaps, this was the real reason why I was put through this test. Future doctoral students would benefit from my experience. It was hard and painful; however, I was reminded of the importance of Resiliency and *RESToration*.

Resiliency and RESToration

Resiliency and RESToration are essential to transformation. Delay does not mean denial! I'm an overcomer. You and I are victorious and we're not victims of any circumstance! When we have setbacks, we can step back, pray, and assess the situation, regroup, be resilient, never give up and press forward.

We can ask, "What's the real message, and what lessons am I to learn during this pivotal moment?" Thankfully, my beloved dad (about whom you will read later in my story) lived to witness online his only daughter walking across the stage to fulfill her dream of becoming a doctor.

Grace and Mercy

During my doctoral program, there were days when I didn't think that I'd be able to accomplish the goals that were set before me. Then, I would remember that I wasn't going to waste the assignment and opportunity God gave me. Furthermore, I was determined not to give up because frankly, I'd invested an enormous amount of time and a lot of money in this program. And, finally, I was not going to let the Lord, myself, my family, and my close friends down.

I'm reminded of the scripture, "*And he said unto me, my grace is sufficient for thee: for my strength is made perfect in weakness. Most gladly, therefore, will I rather glory in my infirmities, that the power of Christ may rest upon me*" (2 Corinthians 12:9, KJV). His strength is perfect. With God, we can do anything. There's really not a need to back down or shy away from our purpose and goals in life. Yes, test and trials will come and go, but indeed what remains the same is the Word of God. The God inside of me served continuously to remind me, "*I can do all things through Christ which strengtheneth me*" (Philippians 4:13, KJV). It's not in our strength, but it's in His strength we are made strong. In His strength, we are perfect because, he guides, provides, and comforts us like no man, woman, or child is capable of doing. He is lovely, and without the Lord and His strength, I am truly nothing.

In many cases, we're not sure when, how, or where these painstaking situations will happen. It's during the "valley seasons" of life where the best lessons are learned. Life lessons tests and trials as described in the Bible,

"My brethren, count it all joy when ye fall into divers temptations; knowing this, that the trying of your faith worketh patience. But let patience have her perfect work, that ye may be perfect and entire, wanting nothing" (James 1:2-4, KJV). Praise the Lord! In the Word of God, there are many promises. As we live a daily life of repentance we can hold on to this truth, *"It is of the Lord's mercies that we are not consumed because his compassions fail not. They are new every morning; great is thy faithfulness"* (Lamentations 3:22-23, KJV).

Transition Flows

A major part of my journey has been about transition. I have found that it's essential to press forward even in the midst of transition. On a daily basis, we encounter amazing and painful family circumstances, financial blessings, and challenges, as well as life-changing world events. On an individual level, a transition can be experienced as the birth of a newborn, finding or losing a loved one, starting or leaving a job or career, buying or selling a home, and so on. Transitions are the passages between the important events and stages of our lives. As we move from one phase to another, a significant amount of change is typically involved. How we enter and exit those life-changing events are just as important.

I would like to share with you how two special individuals changed my life. At the very end of my doctoral journey my biological dad, Tenny Sr., became very sick, and we took on the role of caregiver for both of my beautiful parents. Life, as I had known it to this point, changed drastically. Close to the same time, my dear cousin, who was also my pastor and my "spiritual dad," was promoted to Heaven. Only four months later, my biological dad was also promoted to Heaven. It was painful, losing two wonderful men who meant so much to me—one right after the other. Don't get me wrong, though; I miss them tremendously on Earth, I know they are rejoicing in Heaven, and for this reason, I'm very grateful for the time we shared together.

These two hard-working men imparted some of the most amazing spiritual and life principles into me. They are the epitome of what my story talks about: "Never Give Up—Press Forward." They fulfilled the scripture, *"Fight the good fight of faith, lay hold on eternal life, whereunto thou are also called, and hast professed a good profession before many witnesses"* (I Timothy 6:12, KJV). It's great to know they are with the Father and have joined the great cloud of witnesses in Heaven. Together, they are cheering our entire family, their friends, and church family members on. This is why we (you and I) must never give up, must press forward, and enjoy this sweet precious life journey along the way.

Through the experience of my biological father's death, The Lord reminded me how we will go through phases of change, and in some cases, experience something much like survivor's guilt. On that last Friday morning in September, my mother and I went to hospice to be with my dad. My parents celebrated their 50th anniversary in July, and I felt they needed to spend some time together. When I walked into the room, even though I didn't really know it, I somehow sensed that the end of his life was quickly approaching. After Anetta, my mother, gave her sweet greetings to her husband, it was my turn. I leaned over and said, "Hi, My Daddy. I missed you." He responded in a very weak voice, "I missed you too." I kissed him and shared my favorite words with him. "I love you, Daddy." I wanted so much to see if he was going to say his favorite words back to me. I repeated, "I love you, Daddy," and my dearest dad responded, "I love you back." It took every ounce of strength for me not to break into pieces. To this day, I hold his precious last words close to my heart: "I LOVE YOU BACK."

While my mother and father shared their time together, I waited, and it came to me that I was now being called on to get things in order. I would have to be my mother's strength, and, to do that, I would need the Lord's strength. When the time came, I would be the executrix on behalf of my mother to take care of my father's estate. That's when it became so clear that all of the natural and spiritual training that I had gotten from my two "Dads" was meant for this very hour. It was time to Press Forward! The Holy Spirit immediately strengthened me and started giving me directions on how to move forward.

Truth be told, part of me believed God would heal my dad until the end; however, I intuitively knew preparations were critical and could not be left undone. Mom and I prayed with Dad, went home, and the next morning, as she was preparing to go to an appointment, I told her I wanted to take her to see Dad first. We gathered our things, started walking out the door, and the phone rang. I answered. The hospice nurse said, "Mrs. Simmons, I'm calling to inform you that your father has passed." I looked at Mom, and immediately she knew her beloved husband had taken his flight into eternal life. He was Heaven bound—to be reunited with his Heavenly Father and was undoubtedly happy to join his nephew, other family members, and friends.

My Dad was an energetic, proud, charismatic, outgoing man, who played softball until he was 70. He passed at 71. He loved people, especially his family, but also valued spending time with others: playing ball, piano, and visiting friends in the hospital and nursing home. He also loved his alone time. When we had left hospice the night before, I honestly didn't believe that I would never see him again. But it did cross my mind that, when his time did come, he would want to transition alone. I discerned that he would not want my mom, me, my brothers, or any other family members or friends to witness the final earthly assignment between him and his God.

There were days, for some time afterward, I asked the question: Why didn't I stay to support him through this process? Had I abandoned him in his most important hour? Was I thinking only of myself and the fact that I was blessed to be alive? A form of survivor's guilt raised its ugly head to try and condemn me. But with God's help, I began to cast down any imagination that would allow me to feel guilty or have negative thoughts. God had been in charge of everything and we had all done the very best we could for my dad with the knowledge and resources we had at the time.

I wanted to talk about my two dads because it reminds me of how life will throw curve balls, struggles, disappointments, and failures. But then at the same time, great learnings occur during these crucible, life-changing moments. When a big change happens, we don't know how we are going to respond. All we know is, this thing (you name it) has been thrust like a freight train into our world.

My experience has inspired me to encourage you to not allow sorrow, and self-condemnation to win. As we go through our lives, having dreams, and setting goals and objectives, many people will cross our paths. When a change, such as a loved one leaves for whatever reason, it's essential to have a plan, to have a support system, and to not isolate ourselves.

My immediate and extended family members are some of the most amazing people I know. They are the main members of my support team. We love and support each other. I will never forget the day of my cousin's homegoing celebration, my beautiful cousins (his siblings), aunts, and other family members stopped by the hospital to visit, pray, and spend precious time with my dad. When I think about how my family stopped by the hospital to bless my dad during their personal time of bereavement, I'm still overwhelmed!! This is true LOVE in action! Four months later, all of my beautiful family members helped with my father's celebration. I love them and I'm forever grateful to them! When God guides, He provides—Praise the Lord!

I love the scripture that says, "*I will never leave thee, nor forsake thee*" (Hebrews 13:5, KJV). Dad was never alone; his Lord was with him every step of the way. As I reflect on times in my life when I have felt alone, I realize I have never been alone. For those of you who are reading my story, maybe you haven't yet lost a loved one, but you have experienced loss. Perhaps, you didn't finish an assignment or implement a dream. You disappointed someone who had an expectation of you. Or worse, you didn't reach the very high bar you had set for yourself.

The great news is, it's never too late to 'DREAM BIG'! Set realistic goals and implement your plan of action. I encourage you to use the tools in your toolkit to help you through life-changing situations. Seek spiritual and professional counseling, if needed, and don't be ashamed of your shortcomings and mistakes. Whatever the case or loss, choose today to move forward. Get unstuck! As my dear friend, Kat shares, "Now it's our time to continue to run our race and fulfill our purpose and destiny on earth." Praise God! Our faith, education, life experiences, resource tools, and personal support systemss are what assist us through life-devastating events. Deciding to accept Jesus as my Lord and Savior and believing He is the Son of the Living God, who died for me and my sins (I Corinthians 15:1-3, KJV), and was resurrected from the dead (I Corinthians 15:4, KJV), is my "assurance" that I will reunite with the Lord and see both of my "Dads" again one day in Heaven. If you have tried other solutions and things are not working out, I encourage you to accept Jesus as your personal Lord and Savior, as mentioned above and watch your world transform.

Lessons and Legacy

Over the last twenty years, I've had the wonderful opportunity to serve in ministry, corporations, education, government, community service, and non-profit arenas. As an organizational leader, business consultant, and travel advisor, I have the pleasure of obtaining vital life lessons to assist me in successfully navigating through all of these situations. Here are a few spiritual and professional lessons I've learned that I offer for your consideration:

Relationships Matter. The power of networking and building effective relationships is essential in every area of life. One of my warmest memories during my doctoral journey was the day a group of doctoral candidates met at a restaurant for dinner. Dr. Kathlyeen, myself, and other future doctors were discussing our wonderful education experience and how to support, engage, and encourage other students. Dr. Kathyleen recommended creating an education club, after meeting with Nova's student engagement leader. She was already serving as President for the Student Government Association, so she asked for a volunteer. I said yes to serve as president of the new doctoral education club. The education club hosted weekly meetings on site and virtually served as a platform to assist students with fulfilling their educational goals. As a result, a minimum of ten doctoral students have graduated and there are more future doctors on their way to completing their programs. Effective Relationships Matter!

Prayer and Spiritual Guidance. Prayer and spiritual guidance serve as my personal moral compass. You may wonder how they specifically impact career or organizational success. It is my experience that without a personal relationship with the Lord, all aspects of my life and any assignment, job, or career are far more challenging than they need be. Thus, every day, I begin my morning with prayer and asking for guidance and grace from the Holy Spirit. I also ask the Lord to search my heart and reveal if there is any unforgiveness in my heart or unrepentance. If the answer is yes, I immediately repent, ask for forgiveness, and then I forgive and release others from the situation. When seeking specific professional direction, I pray or have a conversation with God about the issue, ask for wisdom, revelation, and knowledge, and more importantly, I listen! And, if necessary, I pray some more until I receive clarity and direction.

Likewise, our purpose and destiny are linked to people. As individuals, we require water and food to survive naturally. Additionally, it's essential to feed our soul spiritually. I am genuinely grateful for the years I spent learning from my cousin as he taught our family, members, and others the Word of God, (feeding souls spiritually) and how to win souls for the Kingdom of Heaven—this was priceless! If you're not connected to a church home, I would like to encourage you to find a place to worship.

Leading by Example. Identifying and understanding our leadership style serves as a compass for leading others. I lean towards using a Christ-Centered approach to leading individuals courageously, confidently, and most important with compassion. In essence, "Servant Leadership" is my preferred leadership style. Simultaneously, this particular style of leadership is ideal for 'teaching people how to treat you!' Other well-known leaders and authors have said the same thing in different ways. Albert Schweitzer, a winner of the Nobel Peace Prize for his missionary work in Africa, probably said it the most plainly: "The three most important ways to lead people are: by example...by example...by example."

This concept has served me well in navigating successfully in organizations. As a young professional, I would always observe senior leaders. I knew it was important to see what they did, not simply to listen to what they said (Remember, if we are watching our leaders, it is confirmation that other newer or younger professionals are watching us)! Leading by example is a reminder that we are paving the way for future generations.

Mentorship. It goes hand-in-hand with leading by example. Within the first thirty days of any new project, job, or career, I observe and identify the formal and informal leaders in an organization. Once I know who they are, if there is not a formal mentoring program I select one or two among them and ask them to mentor me on the job and in my field. I know they will be the best guides because they have likely been through and accomplished what I am trying to achieve. If Tiger Woods has a coach for every golf swing, I believe it's important for me to have mentors for each area or domain I serve in as well.

Seek Assistance. In addition to mentorship, seek assistance in areas that you know require improvement. Keep things professional, and always remember that it's okay to ask others for help. People share because they care. When feedback is shared, try to refrain from taking things personally. It's my experience that individuals want to help us become successful. If we lack wisdom, understanding, or direction seeking assistance increases our business acumen, skills, and knowledge.

Forgiveness. Forgiveness is essential in life. Sometimes forgiving is tough but necessary for our well-being. Forgiveness brings healing to our souls. I want to offer a solution that has helped me throughout the years. I have learned to forgive God, forgive myself, and forgive those who have offended me. If there is unfinished business, I make it a point to take care of loose ends with the other party (if it's safe and allowed) and move forward. Regardless, I forgive anyway! The world is waiting for you to achieve your goals, objectives, and assignments. You can do it! I believe in you. Allow His strength to guide you through life.

Precious Moments

As I conclude telling you about the journey I took to receive my doctorate, and heart-wrenching life transitions, I find myself thinking about the importance of purpose and destiny. It is our responsibility to leave a footprint for those who will come after us. Fifty years into the future, my prayer is my life's footprint will show these things to be true about me:

- I loved and served my God with all of my heart, soul, and mind.

- I fulfilled, as well as I could. the purpose and destiny to which I was called.

- I stood for holiness, righteousness, integrity, joy, and peace.

- At times, I messed up; however, I applied the lessons learned and moved forward.

- I taught the unadulterated Word of God without fear, compromise, or hesitation in partnership with the Holy Spirit.

- I was chosen to do the unpopular and challenged others to live their best life and walk in love.

- I was a leader of leaders and taught others how to love and live in the secret places—to know Him, to love Him, to follow Him, and to win souls for Him.

- I inspired others to achieve greatness through their gifts and talents.

- I was willing to innovate, rule, and mentor in every domain or area he placed me in for His glory.

- I lived as a woman of wisdom and understanding whose heart belonged to her God.

- I loved and celebrated my friends, and they know they are family to me.

- And last, but not least, my children and grandchildren called me blessed and knew that I loved them unconditionally. My mother will know she is my "role model" for displaying unconditional love and my brothers will always know they are my heroes. And my dear husband believed it was worth everything in the end!

Never Give up ~ Press Forward!

I earnestly trust that my journey, my story of transition and lessons learned, will help and inspire you as you move forward in your endeavors. Life is made up of precious moment. Together, let's intentionally make wonderful memories by helping others to positively change their lives.

"Roadblocks are merely opportunities for solving problems"

-Dr. J. Sabrina Simmons

Acknowledgments

I am humbled and truly grateful to our glorious Father in Heaven, our precious Lord, and Savior Jesus Christ, and the powerful Holy Spirit, who is my closest friend. I am nothing without you and all of Heaven!

I would like to dedicate this chapter to my beloved family. My dad, Tenny R. Smith, Sr., and my spiritual dad and cousin, who inspired, shaped and changed my world. I love and miss you both.

A special thanks to my immediate family: my strong, driven, talented husband Michael and our beautiful, brilliant, and courageous children, Ashley (Nathan), Michael Jr., Erick and our precious grandchildren Destiny, Cason, Camdyn, Katalina, Ahmari, and Ciana. I love you to infinity and beyond! Thank you tremendously from my heart for always loving me and for your continuous support and sacrifice as I run with the vision our Lord has given our family. I am forever grateful to each of you. To my mother and the strongest woman I know, Anetta Smith, who has endured life gracefully and has taught me the true meaning of unconditional love and forgiveness. I love you mom. My brothers, Tenny Smith, Jr., & James Smith, Sr., thanks for always being my protectors and loving me no matter what life throws our way. You are my superheroes! My sister-in-love, Alexis Alexander-Smith, thank you, my love, for always being everything I need and more. My loving best friend for over 20 years, Gwenevere Brinkley, thank you for taking this journey called life with me; I love you to the moon and back!

To all of my extended family members, which are too many to list, I love each of you more than you know! Thank you for always interceding, loving, and standing in the gap for me. The Lord gave our family 'beauty for ashes' with two loving spiritual parents. Thank you to my sweet cousins and Pastor, Apostle Abraham Lincoln, and First Lady, Lisa Washington. I love you and we are forever grateful to you for saying YES, as you continue your assignments in Jacksonville, Florida. A special thanks to my dearest friends, Kat Kerr, Ann Duncan, and Bridget Washington. I'm very humble and grateful to have beautiful friends who I consider family in my life.

Tony Jenkins, you will always be in my eyesight the most wonderful business mentor and friend I could ever ask for in this lifetime. Thank you for always supporting and believing in me! To my dear friend Franklin Givens, WOW! Words cannot express how much I appreciate your gentle, loving approach to business and friendship. Your creative branding and web design work are always fantastic! You and Flora are indeed a divine connection from our Lord. Thank you, dear friends.

Thank you to my innovative photographers, Tenny Rudolph (nephew) and Teraney Wright (goddaughter). Your work is impeccable! *Destiny DeFined* Sisters–You are simply amazing!! I am grateful for our divine connection and assignment.

Lastly, to my amazing editor Barbara Welch words can not express my sincere graditude, thank you my dear friend. My dissertation chairs Dr. Campbell and Dr. Mills, thank you for coaching and encouraging me through this phenomenal journey!!!

~ Dr. J. Sabrina Simmons

Dr. Terri Drummond

Specialty Areas: Leadership, Arbitration, Finance

Dissertation: The Relationship Between Emotional Labor and Job
Satisfaction and Its Effect on Intention to Quit and Quitting Within
Call-Center Environments

Dr. Terri Drummond has served successfully in the capacity of Vice
President for an Automotive Finance Company in Jacksonville, FL. She has
extensive experience in Negotiation, Credit, Collections, Mortgage Lending
and Real Estate. Dr. Drummond has an uncommon complement of financial
management acumen combined with Human Resource and Workforce
Education know-how. Recognized for creating high-performing teams and
leading strategic initiatives, Dr. Drummond's specialty is turning around
underperforming business units. Terri enjoys sharing her vast financial
knowledge by conducting seminars and empowerment workshops.

Dr. Drummond has over 15 years' experience working in Financial
Services. She is very active in the community and has served as a board
member of various local non-profit organizations. Dr. Drummond is
a graduate of Nova Southeastern University with a concentration in
Organizational Leadership. In her personal time, she enjoys volunteering
and learning.

Contact Information:
Email: terridrummond@wediditrway.com

Dr. Kathyleen Gamble-Wyatt

Specialty Areas: Higher Education Administration, Student Success & Mentoring, Change Consulting

Dissertation: A Front-End Analysis on the Perceived Correlation Between Organizational Leadership and Student Success

Dr. Kathyleen Gamble-Wyatt has been employed in a myriad of leadership positions to include academia, finance, and manufacturing. During her tenure as a doctoral student at Nova Southeastern University, Dr. Gamble-Wyatt served in various leadership positions as an integral part of the Student Government Association. Dr. Gamble-Wyatt completed her Doctoral studies majoring in Organizational Leadership with extensive studies in Conflict Resolution. Dr. Gamble-Wyatt's dissertation offered an in-depth research study presenting a Front-End Analysis on the Perceived Correlation Between Organizational Leadership and Student Success. This study has since been published and downloaded by 20 institutions, 22 countries and over 90 readers. Dr. Gamble-Wyatt's ongoing research on student success and leadership is also published in the Distance Learning Journal (V15-1) under the topic, "A Critical Divide in Higher Education: Bridging the Gap Between Student Success and Organizational Leadership." Dr. Gamble-Wyatt's supplemental education attainments include a Master's degree in Public Administration from Georgia Southern University, a B.B.A in Finance from Valdosta State University, and an A.A.S in Accounting from the College of Coastal Georgia.

Dr. Gamble-Wyatt currently resides in Newport News, VA, and is the founder and CEO of Leading Organizational Change Consulting, providing solutions to reorganization and change with minimal disruption to human capital. She is the future publisher of "A Case Management Approach to

Higher Education Administration" and future reader of "Survival Guide for Beginning Educators/Administrators." Dr. Gamble-Wyatt is a lifelong learner who has a passion for education and assisting in furthering the education of others.

Contact Information:

Email: drkgw@wediditrway.com

Email: Leadingchange1231@gmail.com

Business Phone: 904-297-8023

Facebook: Leading Organizational Change Consulting

LinkedIn: www.linkedin.com/in/dr-kathyleen-wyatt-a2055661

Dr. Nicoa Garrett

Specialty Areas: Family Mediator, Community Advocate, Keynote Speaker, Master Facilitator, Consultant, Intimate Partner Violence Expert, Humanitarian, Leadership, Growth & Development Trainer, Content and Curriculum Creator, Real Life Solutions Coach, Mentor, Author

Dissertation: An Investigation of Challenges Facing Black Women in Intimate Partner Violence

Dr. Nicoa Garrett is the founder and owner of Innovative Leadership Solutions, LLC and I AM B.O.S.S. (Builder, Overcomer, Strong & Successful), LLC. She is a Florida Supreme Court Certified Family Mediator as well as a Certified Speaker, Coach, Mentor and Leadership Trainer with the John Maxwell Team. She serves her community as the Co-Chair for the City of Jacksonville Mayor's VAAC (Victim Assistance Advisory) Council. She also serves her community as a member of the Jacksonville Urban League Task Force Committee and as a Master Facilitator for ReClaim Global which helps adult victims of childhood molestation and sexual abuse reclaim their lives.

Dr. Garrett is currently the director of operations for a business in Jacksonville, Florida. She was the former Domestic Violence (DV) Court Coordinator for the 4th Judicial Circuit of Jacksonville, FL, which covers Duval, Clay and Nassau Counties. She trained County Judges, Attorneys, Family Mediators, Court Administration, DV Advocates, Case Managers and community collaborators on domestic violence and its impact on our communities. She received extensive training from the Department of Justice (DOJ) and the Office of Violence Against Women (OVW). She monitored Batterer Intervention Programs (BIP), served on the North Florida Task Force and Fatality Review Teams for many years to ensure policies and procedures were followed to assist victims with resources, guidance and systemic changes. She represented the 4th Judicial Circuit for trainings and collaborations in various states such as Florida, New York, Oregon, New Mexico, Louisiana, Colorado, California, Washington, and Georgia.

Dr. Nicoa Garrett is a native of Detroit, MI, currently residing in Jacksonville, FL. One of her greatest passions is to intentionally cultivate growth in others and help people become effective change agents and great communicators. Her passion is to help others learn how to live life skillfully. She believes in being influential for the purpose of impacting lives, educating, building communities and providing solutions that will ultimately change mindsets that will set people free from barriers.

Dr. Garrett has worked in corporate, financial, institutional, circuit, and faith-based leadership roles for over 30 years. She attended Temple University in Philadelphia, PA, where she received her B.S. in Criminal Justice. She received her M.A. in Information Management & Technology from Webster University in Jacksonville, FL. She received her Ed.D. in Organizational Leadership and Conflict Resolution from Nova Southeastern University.

But that's nothing compared to the love of her life, her HERO and husband of 20 years, and their two beautiful daughters. Dr. Garrett's personal motto is to teach others how to live life fully skilled.

Contact Information:

Email: dr.nicoagarrett@wediditrway.com

Website: www.iam-boss.com

Email: transform@iam-boss.com

Email: ilssolutions1@gmail.com

Facebook: Iamboss Nicoa Garrett

IG: iamboss_nicoagarrett

Twitter: @IAMBOSSNicoa

Dr. Phenessa A. Gray

Specialty Areas: Empowerment, Therapeutic Art Life Coaching, and Social + Emotional Intelligence

Dissertation: Emotional Intelligence: A Phenomenological Study of Successful United States Southern Women Entrepreneurs

Dr. Phenessa A. Gray, native of Jacksonville, FL, is THE Empowerment Doctor. Certified Social+Emotional Intelligence and Therapeutic Art Life Coach, Soulful Creative, Inspirational Author, and Empowerful Spoken Word Artist. She's the Founder and CEO of Bodacious Women Ministries, a non-denominational professional women's group with a passion to serve God & each other as well as Owner of EmpowerCREATIVE! Studios with a mission to empower others to feel better, think better, and create their better world by healing through creative exploration, empowering community with art and soul. She's adept at using empathetic engagement, creative expression, and academic and programmatic expertise in empowering others through arts & crafts (e.g., painting, drawing, jewelry-making, purpose boards, etc.), aromatherapy, collage, computer art, cooking/baking, gardening, interpretive dance, mixed media, photography, and writing (e.g., journaling, poetry, and biblio-coaching). Her educational background includes earning a Bachelor of Arts degree (BA) in English Literature with a minor in Creative Writing from Florida State University; Master of Science in Library Services (MSLS) from Clark Atlanta University; Master of Science in Industrial-Organizational Psychology (MS/IOP) from University of Phoenix; Biblical Counseling Diploma from the American Association of Christian Counselors; Social + Emotional Intelligence Coach Certification from the Institute for Social+Emotional Intelligence; Therapeutic Art Life Coach Certification from Transformation Academy; Thinking for a Change (T4C) Cognitive Behavioral Therapy Intervention Certification from the Jacksonville Sheriff's Office; and, Doctor of Philosophy in Business

Management (PhD) from Capella University. Additionally, Dr. Phenessa has worked in various aspects of leadership including academic, corporate, government, and non-profit settings for the past 20 years.

Dr. Phenessa is a member of Alpha Kappa Alpha Sorority, Inc., Delta Mu Delta International Honor Society in Business, Xi Delta Chapter, and Institute of Social + Emotional Intelligence. Previously, she's served on the Advisory Board, Jacksonville Women's Business Center; past Commissioner and Chair of the Mayor's Commission on the Status of Women; and, past Co-Chair, Fund Development and Board, Jacksonville Sister Cities Association. Also, she has authored and published *Butterfly Expressions Devotional, Grace Gems Devotional, Collisions of the Soul: Into Me See, Inestimable: Poems from a Priceless Soul, and Naked & Unashamed Poetry Album.* She's the proud mother of two beautiful daughters and has a passion for empowering others to be their authentic selves and unleash their unique voices creatively.

Contact Information:

drphenessaagray@wediditrway.com

Facebook: www.facebook.com/empowercr8ive

Instagram: www.instagram.com/empowercr8ive

LinkedIn: www.linkedin.com/in/phenessagray

Facebook: https://www.facebook.com/groups/bodaciouswomenministries

Twitter: www.twitter.com/empowercr8ive

Online Store: https://www.etsy.com/shop/empowercreative

Website: www.EmpowerCREATIVEinc.com

Email: Phenessa@EmpowerCREATIVEinc.com

Angela Malone, MA

Specialty Areas: Counseling/Supervision, Servant Leadership, Employee Engagement Strategist

Dissertation: The Role of Servant Leadership in Fostering Employee Engagement and Job Satisfaction

Angela Malone is a Licensed Mental Health Counselor and owner of Innovation Counseling Center in Jacksonville, FL. As an interactive, holistic-focused therapist, her therapeutic approach is to provide support and practical feedback to help clients effectively address personal life challenges. Angela's areas of expertise include addiction, depression, anxiety, stress, trauma, military issues, couples and marriage difficulties, and women's issues. She integrates complementary methodologies and techniques to offer a highly personalized approach tailored to each client. Angela has been a practicing therapist for 16 years, providing individual, couples, and group therapy. She is a qualified supervisor, providing supervision to unlicensed clinicians seeking to obtain licensure. Angela has been trained in Rapid Resolution Therapy and has specialized training in working with military families and trauma.

Angela is the mother of one daughter and a fur baby named Kash. A member of Delta Sigma Theta, Inc., Angela's educational background includes a B.A. in Criminal Justice from Lane College, an M.S. in Criminal Justice from Southeast Missouri State University, and an M.A. in Counseling from Webster University. She is a current Doctoral candidate at Nova Southeastern University with a concentration in Organizational Leadership. Angela has additional leadership training, which includes graduating from Dale Carnegie's Skills of Success Program, and, in 2019, she will earn her certification in the John Maxwell Team Leadership Program.

Contact Information:

Email: angelamalone@wediditrway.com
Email: amalone@icctransform.com
Website: www.icctransform.com

Dr. J. Sabrina Simmons

Specialty Areas: Author, Speaker, Ministry & Organizational Leader, Travel Advisor

Dissertation: Effects of Mentoring on Career Advancement for Women and People of Color

Dr. J. Sabrina Simmons is a wife, mother, grandmother, and servant who loves to inspire others to live their best life and intentionally live a life of joy, peace, and RESToration. Dr. J. Sabrina has over 20 years of experience in ministry, global business, not-for-profit, and government. She enjoys encouraging others to "Never Give Up and Press Forward." She's an expert in Organizational Leadership, Ministry, Author, Speaker, and Travel Advisor. She enjoys spending time with her family, friends, volunteering, and serving in ministry. When life-changing circumstances and/or significant transitions occur, she believes resiliency and RESToration are essential ingredients needed in our lives to move forward.

Dr. J. Sabrina is the CEO of Limits Off, Inc., and Co-Owner of Limits Off Travel Services. She has a doctoral degree with a concentration focus in Organizational Leadership from Nova Southeastern University; a dual Master of Arts degree in Human Resources Development and Human Resource Management from Webster University; and a bachelor's degree in Workforce Education and Development from Southern Illinois University. She is a past President for the First Coast Diversity Council, and she was appointed by the Mayor as a Commissioner for the Mayor's Commission on the Status of Women in Jacksonville, FL. In addition, she has served on various community organization boards. Dr. J. Sabrina's life work is dedicated to helping individuals positively change their world through fulfilling their purpose and destiny.

Contact Information:

Email: Drjsabrina@wediditrway.com
Email: limitsofforg@gmail.com
Website: www.drjsabrinasimmons.com
Website: www.limitsofftravelservices.com

Gwenevere Cisero Brinkley, MA

Gwen Brinkley has an extensive background in government health services, as well as corporate and nonprofit arenas. She has a dual Master of Arts degree in Human Resources Development and Management from Webster University, a Bachelor's degree in General Business from Jacksonville University, and she is a member of Alpha Kappa Alpha Sorority, Inc.

A servant-leader, Gwen has served on the Board of Directors of numerous not-for-profit organizations, helping the children of the Jacksonville community. She also enjoys spending time with her family and serving in her church ministry.

Contact Information:

Email: gwenbrinkley@wediditrway.com
Email: Contactus@wediditrway.com

Special Thanks

Destiny DeFined Project Manager
Gwenevere Cisero Brinkley, MA

Cover & Book Design
Franklin Givens, Branmarc Design, Inc.

Photographers
James Schlefstein, HiDef Pixel, Jacksonville Beach, FL
TSC Video & Photography Productions, Newport News, VA
Tenny Rudolph Photography, Jacksonville, FL

Hair & Makeup Artist
Kimberley Jacques of Kimmy's Touch (Kimmystouch.com)
Andrea Silky Hoilett, Hair Stylist
Platinum Stylz, Newport News, VA
Waynette Williams, Jacksonville, FL
Lady Pamela Kirkpatrick, Jacksonville, FL

What's Your "R"

Notes

References

Davis, Angela (n.d.). AZQuotes.com. Retrieved July 25, 2019, from AZQuotes.com Web site: https://www.azquotes.com/author/3699-Angela_Davis

Hughes, Langston. "Dream Defined (Harlem)." Poetryfoundation. org. The Poetry Foundation. 07 May 2013, retrieved from https://www.poetryfoundation.org

Peck, M. S. (1997). The road less traveled and beyond: [large print]: Spiritual growth in an age of anxiety. Thorndike, ME: Thorndike.

Radiant. In The Oxford English dictionary (3rd edition). Retrieved from https://www.lexico.com/en/definition/radiant

Shakespeare, W., 1564-1616. (1994). The merchant of Venice. Harlow, Essex, England: Longman.

Made in the USA
Lexington, KY
12 November 2019

56928146R00083